INSIDE THE MULTINATIONALS

THE ECONOMICS OF INTERNAL MARKETS

ALAN M. RUGMAN

New York Columbia University Press 1981

Printed and bound in Great Britain

CONTENTS

To my parents

TABLES AND FIGURES

Figures

Tables

PREFACE

Conceived at Columbia University, New York, developed and expanded in Montreal, Quebec and finally brought to fruition in Halifax, Nova Scotia, this book reflects the varied nature of its subject matter – the multinational enterprise. Yet it belongs to none of these places. Rather the genesis of the central idea in this book is the University of Reading in England, where I first developed an interest in the concept of internalization. There the work of John Dunning and Mark Casson and the frequent visitors to the international business side of the economics department has developed an oral tradition of analysis of the multinational enterprise (MNE). In this oral tradition, the internalization of markets as a theoretical rationale for the MNE was becoming a central concept by the academic year 1976 to 1977, which I spent there as a Visiting Research Fellow. The Reading oral tradition has been supplemented by the influential series of Reading 'greenbacks', edited by Professor Dunning, where the elements of internalization are sketched out in issues over the last several years. I am grateful to him for very helpful suggestions and to Mark Casson for many stimulating conversations and for consenting to write the Foreword.

When teaching international business at Columbia University from 1978 to 1979 it became clear to me that internalization is a unifying paradigm for the theory of foreign direct investment (FDI). In reviewing the literature on the determinants of FDI I found that each scholar is writing about one or another market imperfection, which induces the MNE to use an internal market. This analysis is the cornerstone of this book. Yet there are situations in which internalization is not the most efficient response to a market imperfection. In one of the chapters here Ian Giddy and I consider alternatives to internalization, such as exporting and licensing. We explore the conditions under which each one of these modes of servicing a foreign market is optimal at certain points of time, and how the choice of modality may vary over time. The materials in Chapter 3 were developed jointly with Ian Giddy, although the use of them here is my responsibility.

While in the finance department of Concordia University, Montreal, I wrote the chapters which apply internalization to financial aspects of MNEs and to multinational banking. The applications of internalization to Canadian policy issues, namely the transfer of technology between the US and Canada and the issue of regulation of the MNE, were commenced during the period spent in Quebec but completed at Dalhousie. Preparation of the final draft of this book was facilitated by the Centre for International Business Studies at Dalhousie University.

Turning to other specific intellectual debts, I have received helpful comments on Chapter 2 by Winston Brown, Mark Casson, John Dunning, Ian Giddy, Stefan Robock and Raymond Vernon. A previous version of this chapter was presented at the Eastern Economic Association meeting in Boston, May 1979.

For the first half of Chapter 3, on modes of entry to a foreign market, written jointly with Ian Giddy, useful comments were received from Mark Casson, Bernie Wolf, Hugh Neuberger, Larry Kryznowski, Sylvester Damus, Sandra Dow, Evan Douglas, Robert Grosse, Rebecca Klemm and members of seminars at Columbia, Miami and Dallas. Part of the chapter was presented at the annual meetings of the North American Economic Studies Association at Atlanta in December 1979 and the rest revised in late 1980.

The work on implications of internalization for international finance in Chapter 4 was improved by helpful comments from Solomaz Ayarslan, Gary Craig, Ian Giddy, Gunter Dufey and Kenneth Riener. A previous version of this chapter was presented at the annual meetings of the Financial Management Association in Boston in October 1979.

Chapter 5 benefited from comments by Ian Giddy, James Dean, Jack Galbraith and James Desreumaux. Research assistance was provided by Penny Ellison, who prepared the tables used here for her MBA research paper at Concordia University, 1979-80.

Work on Chapter 6 dealing with the transfer of technology to Canada was supported by a grant from the Tenth Associates' Workshop in Business Research of the University of Western Ontario. Under this fellowship I am pleased to acknowledge the help of Terry Deutscher and the research assistance of Roland Ghanem. Helpful comments on this technology transfer chapter have been provided by Judith Alexander, Evan Douglas, Gary Hewitt, Danny Shapiro, Harold Crookell, Peter Killing, Don Lecraw and others at Western Ontario and by members of seminars at Dalhousie and Western. Other versions of this chapter were presented at the annual meetings of the North American Economic Studies Association in Denver, Colorado in September 1980, and at the European International Business Association Annual Conference in Antwerp, December 1980.

A previous version of Chapter 7 was presented to a Conference on the Transnational Corporation hosted by the University of Sudbury, October 1980. In this chapter research assistance has been provided by Mara Crassweller, one of the Student Fellowship holders of the Centre for International Business Studies of Dalhousie University.

The manuscript was helped along at Concordia University by Susan Regan, Susan Altimas and Lorraine Vineberg. It was prepared and typed in its final form by Pat Zwicker, Centre for International Business Studies at Dalhousie University.

Helen Rugman did most of the proofreading of the numerous drafts of the manuscript and helped prepare the bibliography and index.

I am grateful to all these people for their help and advice in the completion of this project. Their comments and interest in my work have been of great value in making my thinking and writing more precise. The remaining errors in this book are my responsibility alone.

Alan M. Rugman
Centre for International
Business Studies
Dalhousie University

ACKNOWLEDGEMENTS

For granting permission to reproduce his materials published elsewhere the author thanks the following journals:

Chapter 2: 'Internalization as a General Theory of Foreign Direct Investment: A Re-Appraisal of the Literature,' *Weltwirtschaftliches Archiv (Review of World Economics)* vol. 116, no. 2 (Tubingen: J.C.B. Mohr, June 1980): 365-79.

Chapter 4: 'Implications of Internalization for Corporate International Finance,' *California Management Review* vol. 23, no. 2 (Winter 1980): 73-9. Reprinted by permission of the Regents of the University of California.

Chapter 7: Book review of Tamir Agmon and Charles P. Kindleberger, eds. *Multinationals from Small Countries*. Cambridge, Mass.: MIT Press, 1977. From *Economic Development and Cultural Change* vol. 28, no. 4 (July 1980): 871-5.

FOREWORD

There is now a vast literature on the multinational enterprise (MNE) and the related subject of foreign direct investment. Much of the literature consists of case studies of particular firms operating in particular host economies. To interpret the results of these case studies correctly it is necessary to have a satisfactory theory of the MNE, and until recently such a theory was lacking. Alan Rugman has played a major role in the development of this theory, and it is a pleasure to see his work made available to a wider audience through this book.

There are three major problems facing anyone who attempts to theorize about the MNE. The first is that the subject is interdisciplinary. Understanding of the MNE requires a grasp not only of economic theory, but of the theory of finance as well. Within economics, it is necessary to draw upon both the theory of international trade and the theory of industrial organization. Alan Rugman has a detailed knowledge of all these areas, and this has enabled him to provide a balanced perspective on the MNE.

Secondly, the complexities of the MNE mean that the theorist must tread a careful path between oversimplification on the one hand, and a preoccupation with minor detail on the other. A major pitfall when theorizing is to try to take account of too many different phenomena at once. This mistake is very common in international economics, and particularly so in studies of the MNE. Some theorists are overambitious, and range too widely to do full justice to any one aspect of their subject. Their work frequently degenerates into mere taxonomy. They list all the factors which could conceivably influence the MNE, demonstrate the multifarious ways in which these factors interact, and conclude by listing all possible outcomes which could result from these interactions.

There is no doubt that taxonomy is valuable as a preliminary to theorizing. It provides an analytical framework which ensures that the concepts and definitions are mutually consistent. But it is not a substitute for theorizing itself. Taxonomies can only explain the real world in a very limited way, either by pigeon-holing observed phenomena within the categories defined by the taxonomy, or by telling anecdotes illustrative of the possibilities they raise.

Ultimately, the weakness of taxonomy is that everything is possible;

the taxonomy provides labels for real world events, but gives no predictions of them. Predictions are obtained by imposing restrictions on the taxonomy—by postulating that certain cases identified by the taxonomy will never be observed.

Alan Rugman is a theorist, not a taxonomist. He draws his inspiration from the theory of efficient markets. The predictions of this theory stem from the postulate that no two individuals will forego a mutually beneficial opportunity for trade. Trade proceeds up to the point where no one can be made better off without someone else being made worse off; in the jargon of the economist, the allocation of resources is Pareto-efficient. This insight into economic behaviour has proved very successful in many fields of inquiry, and the theory of the MNE is no exception.

This brings us to the third problem facing the student of the MNE. Orthodox economic theory has been developed on the assumption that there are no transaction costs. But as recent work has shown, transaction costs are fundamental to the theory of the MNE—indeed to the theory of the firm itself. In a world of no transaction costs the rationale for the firm is unclear. To explain the existence of the MNE it is necessary to introduce transaction costs into conventional economic theory. In this respect students of the MNE have become theoretical innovators.

However, conventional theory affords a number of important insights into economic behaviour, and it is important not to lose sight of these in the course of modifying the theory. One of the great strengths of Alan Rugman's work is that in expounding the theory of the MNE he keeps these insights to the fore, and builds the theory around them. This gives his exposition a coherence which is lacking in many other works on the MNE.

As noted above, it is the introduction of transaction costs that links conventional theory to the theory of the MNE. The important point is that transaction costs vary according to the kind of market institution used. The relative costs of alternative institutional arrangements influence the choice of market institution. Competition tends to lead to the selection of the most efficient market institution. Where international technology transfer, and international trade in intermediate products are concerned, the most efficient institution is often the MNE.

The introduction of transaction costs into economic theory is sometimes seen as complicating matters and removing most of the theory's predictive power. Nothing could be further from the truth. Certainly, the introduction of transaction costs removes some of the more absurd counterfactual predictions of the theory. But at the same time it generates a wealth of new predictions which explain phenomena – such as the MNE – about which the orthodox theory has nothing interesting to say.

The proposition that individuals will seek out mutually beneficial trading opportunities still applies when there are transaction costs. But now trade takes place only up to the margin where the gain from additional trade is just equal to the additional transaction cost involved. In the long run it does not matter who actually incurs the transaction cost – the buyer or the seller – for this will be reflected in the negotiated price: ultimately the incidence of the transaction costs on the two parties will be determined solely by the competitive conditions that prevail. (However, this result no longer applies if there are externalities, so that some of the transaction costs are borne by those who are not party to the transaction.)

A second postulate can now be introduced: namely that transactors have a mutual interest in reducing transaction costs, and so will collaborate in seeking out least-cost methods of transaction. The firm is an institution for minimizing transaction costs. The reason why managers control the allocation of resources within the firm is that it is too expensive to negotiate separately over every single activity that needs to be performed. This accounts for a number of aspects of corporate behaviour which are so familiar that they are usually just taken for granted.

It explains why employment contracts give management discretion over the deployment of workers between various tasks, instead of specifying the precise tasks that each worker must perform under each set of possible circumstances. The use of a single contract of employment in place of multifarious contracts for specific tasks reduces the number of transactions involved in the employment of labour, and so economizes on transaction costs in the labour market.

The same principle explains why firms own physical assets rather than hire them, or buy specific asset-services from independent asset-owners. It is cheaper to own rather than to hire because ownership of the asset secures a continuous stream of future asset-services with a single transaction – the purchase of the asset – while if the same stream of services were hired, the contract of hire would periodically have to be renegotiated and renewed – involving several separate transactions. It is cheaper to hire rather than to purchase specific asset-services because the hirer obtains a range of possible uses of the asset without having to negotiate separately over each of these uses.

The minimization of transaction costs also implies that

complementary assets, when utilized together, should have a common owner, so that their use can be co-ordinated not by negotiation but by control. Sometimes complementarity is fully exploited only when the assets are physically adjacent to each other – this is the case of plant economies in production. In other cases complementarity can be exploited at a distance. This is exemplified by the geographical division of labour in production: different assets are at different locations, and are connected by flows of intermediate products, e.g. flows of components, semi-processed materials, even proprietary know-how. Complementarity at a distance is associated with multiplant economies. Multiplant operations that span national boundaries generate MNEs.

The rationale for the MNE is that it reduces transaction costs by buying up complementary assets located in different nations and integrating their operations within a single unit of control. In doing so it creates an 'internal market' for the intermediate products. The concept of an internal market is particularly apt if administration within the firm is decentralized, with powers of control being delegated to the managers of individual plants. In this case control over the intermediate product actually changes hands as the product moves between plants, though ownership of the product does not.

But it is change of ownership, rather than change of control, which is mainly responsible for transaction costs. Change of ownership creates an incentive for both parties to haggle over the price, for where change of ownership is involved it is price which determines the distribution of the gains from trade. Change of ownership also creates an incentive to default, for each party gains most if the other party fulfils his obligations, but they themselves do not. Neither of these incentives occurs in an internal market; it is for this reason that in many instances an internal market is a more efficient institution for allocating resources than is an external one.

The predictive power of the internalization theory may be illustrated in the following way. Assume that each market has a set-up cost, incurred in bringing buyers and sellers together, or otherwise establishing channels of communication between them. There is also a variable cost associated with negotiating and enforcing each transaction. This variable cost is independent of the value of the transaction. However, there is a maximum quantity that can be transacted at any one time, for example, all transactions may have to be effected spot, and there may be a maximum bulk sale that the physical storage and distribution system can accommodate. Suppose that this maximum quantity is fairly small, so that variations in the quantity traded in the market have to be accommodated by variations in the number of transactions. It follows that the total variable cost is directly proportional to the quantity traded.

Consider an intermediate product market linking two stages of a vertical production process, and suppose that there is just one plant producing at each stage of the process. Assuming no barriers to either take-over, merger or divestment, equilibrium in the equity market requires that the joint profits of the two plants are maximized. Given the cost function of the selling plant and the cost and revenue functions of the buying plant, the contribution of intermediate product trade to the joint profits of the two plants can be derived; it is illustrated by the curve AA^1 in Figure 0.1, which peaks at B. In the absence of transaction costs B determines the equilibrium volume of trade q_0.

Suppose now that the establishment of an internal market incurs greater set-up costs than the establishment of an external market. The cost of the internal market may be identified with the cost of taking over both plants and establishing an integrated system of control. By comparison, the set-up cost of the external market is negligible. However the internal market has much lower variable costs than the external market because there is less incentive to haggle and default. The transaction costs of the internal market are illustrated by the locus CC^1 while the costs of the external market are illustrated by the locus DD^1; it can be seen that CC^1 has a larger intercept and a lower slope than DD^1.

The lines CC^1 and DD^1 intersect at E. To the left of E the external market has the lowest transaction costs, and so the minimum transaction cost is indicated by the segment DE. To the right of E the internal market has the lowest transaction cost, and so the minimum transaction cost is indicated by the segment EC^1. Thus overall, the minimum transaction cost is indicated by the locus DEC^1, which has a kink at E, corresponding to the volume of trade q_1. At quantities below q_1 the plants will be separately owned, and will trade at arm's length, while above q_1 the plants will be integrated and trade will be internalised.

Whether the market is actually internal or external depends upon the volume of trade, and this in turn depends upon the way both the gains from trade and minimum transaction cost vary with the quantity traded. Profits, measured by the gains from trade net of transaction costs, are represented by the vertical discrepancy between AA^1 and DEC^1. They are measured in the figure FF^1, which peaks at G, giving a profit-maximizing output q_2. Since in this example $q_2 > q_1$, the market is internalized.

One obvious prediction of this theory is that the propensity to internalize is greater the greater is the volume of trade between the two plants. However it should be emphasized that this result depends upon

Figure 0.1: Transaction Costs of Internal and External Markets

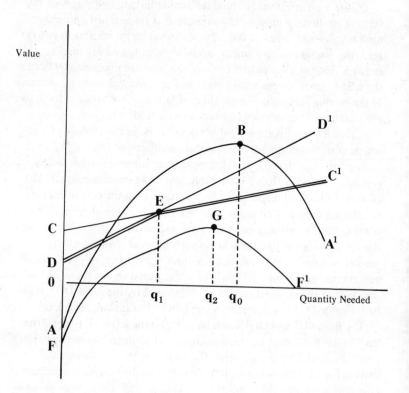

a large volume of trade being associated with a high frequency of transactions in the external market. If the frequency of transactions could be reduced, either by long-term contracts, or by purchasing more occasionally in greater bulk, then the incentive to internalize would diminish. Thus the theory predicts that not only the volume of trade, but also the scope for long-term contracts and for bulk-buying, will influence the degree of internalization.

At present it is possible to test these predictions only in terms of anecdotal evidence, but the results are nevertheless quite encouraging. For example, when applied to the market for technical know-how, the theory predicts that firms with large-scale R and D producing a con-tinuous stream of innovations are more likely to internalize them than is a firm with a smaller R and D effort, whose innovations are essentially 'one-off'. Thus foreign direct investment is most likely to be associated with large-scale R and D activity, and licensing with small-scale R and D activity.

Similarly, firms selling high-quality branded products are likely to purchase regularly from a small number of high-quality component or raw material producers, while firms selling unbranded products are more likely to shop around the world markets for the cheapest supplies, since they have less goodwill to lose if the quality they sell is poor. Because of their frequent purchases from the same suppliers the brand operators have a greater incentive to internalize through backward integration. The theory therefore predicts that foreign direct investment in component production or raw material extraction will be more common among suppliers of branded products than among suppliers of unbranded products.

In both these examples there are, of course, other factors at work besides the ones stated by the theory. The point to be emphasized is that a general theory of transaction costs does exist, and that this theory is very rich in predictions about the role of internal and external markets in a competitive economy. The theory of the MNE, as developed by Alan Rugman and others, testifies to its considerable potential in just one area of economics. At present, this is the best-developed area of the theory. It is to be hoped that these insights will soon be applied to other areas of economics. I believe that Alan Rugman's book, by emphasizing the generality of the theory, will expedite this process.

Mark Casson
University of Reading

1 MULTINATIONALS AND THE NEW THEORY OF INTERNALIZATION

Introduction

In the past ten years or so it has become academically respectable to study the multinational enterprise. There is now a sufficient body of high-quality analytical work available to develop a theory of the multinational enterprise (MNE). The sophisticated theoretical models of recent years have been accompanied by more detailed and complex empirical studies of foreign direct investment. The time has come to integrate this theoretical and empirical work into a general theory of the MNE.

The theory of internalization is now being recognized by a growing body of scholars as such a general theory of foreign direct investment. This book explains why the MNE uses its internal market to service foreign markets with its firm specific advantage in knowledge or other proprietary information. The implications of internalization theory are explored. It is demonstrated that an appropriate synthesis of the literature on market imperfections in an international context can be built upon the foundation of internalization theory.

While the emphasis in this book is upon the economics of foreign direct investment it is hoped that the theory of the MNE developed here can be used by those working in the general field of international business. Internalization stems from economics but it is a concept with potential applications across disciplines, since it is a fundamental explanation of the rationale for the MNE.

Multinational enterprises and internal markets go together. The internal market is the device which makes the multinational enterprise the dominant force it is in today's world. The driving force of the MNE, the internal market, warrants more attention than it has received in the past. The large and growing literature on the MNE, and especially on the theory of the MNE, has neglected internalization until fairly recently. In this book the concept of internalization is explored in detail and its implications are extended to a greater degree than has been possible before.

The plan of the book is straightforward. This chapter introduces the topic of internalization and relates it to the current performance of the MNE. Definitions of the MNE and of internalization are given. The area focus of the book, which makes special reference to Canada is explained and defended as a relevant case study. Chapter 2 explores the literature of the theory of the MNE in order to develop the central argument of this book, namely that internalization is a general theory of foreign direct investment (FDI). Chapter 3 examines the conditions under which the MNE chooses between three methods of servicing foreign markets; exporting, FDI and licensing. The choice of modality is examined in a one period and dynamic context.

With this theoretical foundation established the remainder of the book examines implications of internalization. Chapter 4 applies internalization theory to such areas of corporate international finance as foreign exchange risk, international diversification, transfer pricing and the finance function of the MNE. Chapter 5 draws out the implications of internalization for multinational banking and examines evidence on the changing profitability of Canadian banks as their degree of multinationality has increased. Chapter 6 applies the concept of internalization to the transfer of technology to advanced nations such as Canada. Empirical work on the difference in R and D by multinational and domestic firms is reported and interpreted. Chapter 7 asks the question: should the MNE be regulated? It is answered in the context of both an advanced nation such as Canada, and also from the viewpoint of less developed nations.

As the distinctive organization of the modern international economy the MNE needs to be examined in this careful and detailed fashion. The focus of this book upon the internal markets of the MNE is an economic one. The MNE is basically an economic animal. Its mission is to produce and market goods on a worldwide basis. This economic function is facilitated by the use of its internal market. While the MNE is a powerful actor in the international arena, its political and social impacts are largely ignored in this book, not because these are unimportant, but due to my belief that it is a greater priority to examine the essential economic elements of the MNE. The principle of internalization developed here can be applied to the dimensions beyond economics at a later stage. The economic implications of internalization theory are of sufficient importance to stand alone and the theory is valuable in its own right.

The Application of Economic Theory to International Investment

It can be shown in economic theory that the market mechanism will allocate goods and services efficiently in any economy. In terms of a general equilibrium model all production and consumption decisions can theoretically be solved by following the well known micro efficiency conditions. Indeed the general equilibrium approach can be applied just as well in a totally planned economy, the only modification being that 'shadow' prices have to be computed instead of using market determined prices.

One of the major implications of general equilibrium theory is that any imperfections in the goods, factor or consumption markets will inevitably lead to some reduction in social welfare. Such imperfections may be:

(a)   in the factor market such as a trade union which raises the money wages of some workers above their marginal value product,

(b)   a government tax on capital which prevents equality between the rate of return and marginal physical product of capital,

(c)   an externality in either the product or consumption market in which there is a divergence between the private and social costs, for example in pricing pollution or knowledge.

These examples of market failure prevent the efficient allocation and consumption of goods and factors in terms of the general equilibrium model of neoclassical economic theory.

Using the foregoing summary statement of economic theory it is possible to apply the general principle of efficiency to an analysis of contemporary problems of international business. Such problems are, in general, in the areas of: the theory and regulation of multinational enterprises, technology transfer, taxation and transfer pricing, and corporate international finance. In all of these areas the international economy is characterized by market imperfections. The welfare costs of such distortions can be calculated in an approximate fashion, and such estimates will provide a useful indicator of the costs of such problems. This approach does not show that all market imperfections should be removed, as this would be an impossible task given the institutional parameters facing a policy maker in the field of international business. The value of this focus upon efficiency is to demonstrate the analytical issues of international business in a clearer light.

The general equilibrium approach has been used in trade theory. In a definitive study Max Corden (1974), for example, applied the theory of distortions (developed in the trade literature since the mid-1960s) to an analysis of international trade problems. In general his major principles are these:

(a)   a tariff is inferior to free trade,
(b)   a tax subsidy system is superior to a tariff but itself is inferior to free trade,
(c)   free trade is always best.

While these principles have been applied elegantly and convincingly in the study of trade policy, it remains to refine the theoretical tools, and to apply them, in the field of international business. The MNE is waiting for analysis.

To summarize, the main implication from economic theory is that the market mechanism can allocate goods and factors efficiently. Any market imperfections will have welfare costs, and in general public policy should be directed towards minimizing such costs. Unfortunately most policy in the international business area worsens the distortions rather than correcting them. In addition policies are often implemented in separate sectors and the spillover effects of these policies are frequently overlooked. The general equilibrium model recognizes the interdependent forces of the economy. Using it as a basic tool in the analysis of international business will focus attention upon interdependencies in the world economy.

Internationalization versus Internalization

In recent years the theory of the multinational enterprise has been substantially modified to incorporate elements from the disciplines of economics and international finance. These inputs complement and to some extent replace the traditional managerial approach to international business. This book summarizes both the traditional and newer explanations of international activity, and suggests an appropriate synthesis, namely the theory of internalization.

The traditional managerial explanations of international business have focused upon the additional risks facing a firm as it goes abroad. The theories attempt to explain the appropriate entry strategies to be followed by a multinational enterprise or exporting firm. One of the most influential explanations of international business has been put forward by Professor Aharoni (1966). He suggests the following stages of entry into foreign markets:

(a)   licensing,
(b)   exporting,
(c)   establishment of local warehouses and direct local sales,
(d)   local assembly and packaging,
(e)   formation of a joint venture,
(f)   foreign direct investment (that is, full scale local production and marketing by a wholly owned subsidiary).

This description of the entry strategies of a typical firm engaged in international business is based on the assumption that foreign operations are risky. This managerial approach deals with the international business decision as an extension of the domestic business decision. That is, it is assumed that a firm goes abroad only to expand its market, selling and producing abroad similar goods to those it has manufactured for its domestic market. The firm engages in the process of internationalization in several stages, initially preferring to sell its goods abroad through licensing arrangements or by exporting, and only at a later stage even setting up marketing offices. Only at a very late stage will it consider producing abroad or the formation of a joint venture. It was thought that as the depth of involvement increased the risk facing the firm from its international operations would increase. In practice this assumption has been questioned, and an alternative explanation has been developed.

The new explanation of the activities of multinational firms makes use of the theory of internalization. The theory of internalization suggests that a firm considers explicitly the relative costs of servicing foreign markets in one of three possible ways. First, the firm may simply wish to export to foreign markets. Secondly, the firm may engage in foreign direct investment, that is, set up an overseas subsidiary to produce for a local market. Thirdly, a firm may wish to license to a possible host-country producer. The method of servicing a foreign market may change over time, as the various costs associated with each of these three strategies change. Therefore, it is necessary to consider explicitly the additional costs of servicing a foreign market by exporting, the additional costs of servicing a foreign market by foreign direct investment, and the possible costs associated with dissipation of the firm's knowledge advantage once licensing is considered as the third option.

A recent paper, see Rugman (1980c), contrasts the managerial or marketing theory of internationalization with the theory of internalization. The latter theory has been developed by economists, especially

those associated with the 'Reading School' in England. It is demonstrated that internalization is a general theory of foreign direct
investment, and that the traditional approach which emphasizes
internationalization, is in need of some rethinking.

The essence of internalization theory is the recognition of market
imperfections which prevent the efficient operation of international
trade and investment. It shows that the multinational enterprise (MNE)
has developed in response to exogenous government induced regulations
and controls which negated the theoretical rationale for free trade and
private foreign investment as explanations of international trade and
investment. The process of internalization permits the MNE to overcome the externalities resulting from such regulations.

In addition, the MNE has been an efficient response to non-
government market failure in areas such as information and knowledge.
Here the MNE can use its firm specific advantage in knowledge and
technology to service foreign markets by internal production and
marketing rather than through exporting or licensing. The latter two
options are denied the MNE, due to the risk of dissipation of its firm
specific advantage. In general, the MNE is in the business of bypassing
externalities by creating an internal market to replace missing external
markets.

In his seminal article Coase (1937) showed that a domestic corporation
may bypass the regular market and use internal prices to overcome the
excessive transactions costs of an outside market. Hymer (1976) applied
the theory of industrial organization and imperfect markets to explain
the MNE. Caves (1974) relates trade theory to imperfect markets and
FDI. The first explicit treatment of the relationship between market
imperfections and internalization is in Buckley and Casson (1976).
There is also an excellent synthesis of the literature on the MNE, built
around the concept of internalization, in Dunning (1977), although he
prefers an eclectic approach to explain FDI. The work of Buckley and
Casson is related to Vernon's product cycle model in Giddy (1978). A
recent rigorous treatment of internalization appears in Casson (1979),
while the next chapter explores the role of this new theory as a unifying
paradigm for FDI.

This book will attempt to introduce the concept of internalization,
and to explore some of its implications for international business theory.
The next chapter attempts a more detailed explanation of internalization
theory, building upon the major works identified in the literature by
type of market imperfection. This chapter serves to introduce the point
that the foreign investment decision is a decision made by the

multinational enterprise, and that the rationale for this particular form of international institution is the theory of internalization.

This new general theory of foreign direct investment explains why the multinational enterprise will choose to service foreign markets by subsidiary production, rather than by such alternative modes as exporting, licensing or joint ventures. It incorporates elements from other disciplines than economics and can be used as a building block for the work of scholars from different backgrounds, see Rugman's paper in Negandhi (1980). Internalization theory brings analytical precision to the foreign investment decision. It permits a firm to make a precise choice of mode of entry, and to reappraise its choice as exogenous parameters change over time. Internalization can become the central concept of international business and is already the core of any theory of foreign direct investment.

Definition of Internalization

Internalization is the process of making a market within a firm. The internal market of the firm substitutes for the missing regular (or external) market and solves the problems of allocation and distribution by the use of administrative fiat. The internal prices (or transfer prices) of the firm lubricate the organization and permit the internal market to function as efficiently as a potential (but unrealized) regular market.

Whenever there is a missing market (as in the pricing of intermediate products such as knowledge), or when the transactions costs of the regular market are excessive, then there will be a reason for internalization. Since the economy is characterized by many such market imperfections there is always a strong motivation for firms to create internal markets. On a worldwide basis there are countless barriers to trade and other market imperfections so there are even stronger reasons for the emergence of multinational enterprises. Such firms internalize international market imperfections (as well as domestic ones) and thereby increase global social welfare.

Internalization is a theory of the multinational enterprise since it encompasses within itself the reasons for international (as well as domestic) production. A firm will wish to locate itself abroad to gain access to foreign markets. It will choose foreign direct investment when exporting and licensing are unreliable, inferior, or more costly options. Internalization is a device for keeping a firm specific advantage over a worldwide scale. The multinational enterprise is an organization that is able to monitor the use of its firm specific advantage in knowledge by establishing abroad miniature replicas of the parent firm. These foreign subsidiaries supply each foreign market and permit the multinational to segment national markets and use price discrimination to maximize worldwide profits. Internalization allows the multinational to control its affiliates and to regulate the use of the system specific advantage on a global basis.

An internal market is a valuable asset to the firm and it seeks to protect this advantage by ongoing R and D in order to generate new waves of technological advantage. This requires centralization of the R and D function, or very careful control of and integrated planning of offshore innovations, since the latter may be hard to market within the multinational firm if another part of the system, such as the finance function, is centralized. The ownership of a knowledge asset is best protected within the management structure of a multinational enterprise. It is a system that is organized to administer the advantage efficiently and the most likely method of control will be a centralized one, although there are some exceptions to this general rule. The multinational enterprise is, in general, a remarkable institutional response to both the natural market failure in knowledge and other intangible products; and also to the market imperfections erected by government regulations and tariffs.

Internalization demonstrates that it is always possible to make a market. The dominance of multinational enterprises in today's world economy confirms the predictive ability of internalization theory. Nowhere is the role of multinationals more noticeable than in Canada, so this nation is used as a case study throughout the book to highlight the practical relevance of internalization theory. All of the implications of internalization are applicable to other advanced, and less developed, nations so the references to Canada can be regarded as illustrative rather than definitive. Further aspects of the definition of internalization will be reserved for later parts of the book. The definition will be extended in the context of the particular subject under examination.

The internal market of the MNE is an international extension of the new theory of the firm developed in a domestic context, most recently by Williamson (1975). He has shown that the internal market of a firm is responsive to conditions of imperfect information and that firms are hierarchical and centralized. Related work on vertical integration and on the organization of internal markets develops the point that centralized decision making is made by the firm. Resource allocation processes that are internalized are those carried out in a centralized manner.

Williamson's book highlights the complexities that result when internal decisions of the firm are centralized. Thus the theory of internalization is also a theory of centralization in decision making (including applications to the R and D function of the MNE).

Definition of MNE and Area Focus

Scholars in the field of international business and economics define a multinational enterprise as either (a) having subsidiaries in one, six or more nations, or (b) having a ratio of foreign (F) to total (T) operations (i.e. sales, employees, etc.) greater than some arbitrary number, e.g. (F/T) > 10 per cent or (F/T) > 25 per cent etc.

The first definition is used by those associated with the Harvard multinational enterprise project, such as Vernon (1971). Dunning (1973) and Hood and Young (1979) also use the first method since the essence of being multinational is international *production.* Otherwise foreign markets could be serviced by exports and trade theory would suffice to explain world supply and consumption matters. Bruck and Lees (1968), the United Nations study (1978) and Rugman (1976) use the second. The problem with the (F/T) ratio is that it includes exports as well as sub-sidiary production, so it has to be used carefully. It is, however, especially useful in financial analysis, since it captures the total foreign effect on domestic share prices.

The Perlmutter (1969) model is derived from behavioural theory and management science rather than economics. Not surprisingly it does not emphasize that the unique aspect of being multinational is inter-national production, as it should. Instead, the definitions of firms as ethnocentric (home oriented), polycentric (host oriented) or geocentric (worldwide oriented) describe a management philosophy only. Yet managers need to be evaluated on their performance rather than their attitudes, since the latter are unimportant in themselves. For example, while an ethnocentric firm is clearly non-multinational, either a poly-centric or a geocentric firm could have many foreign subsidiaries and thus qualify as a multinational on the grounds of international pro-duction. A distinction between these latter two groups is of little value in defining multinationality.

In this book I use the term 'multinational enterprise' (MNE) on all occasions. This is a theoretically more appropriate term than 'trans-national corporation' for the purposes of the analysis used in this study.

For a devastating critique of the misuse of the term 'transnational

corporation' see Milton Hochmuth (1978). He reviews the development
of the bastard terminology and reveals that its adoption by the UN even
ran counter to the recommendation of its own Group of Eminent
Persons who advocated the term 'transnational enterprise'. They defined
multinational corporations as 'enterprises which own or control production in service facilities outside the country in which they are based'.
This is an economist's definition, and was heavily influenced by the
membership of Professor John Dunning in the group.

The term 'transnational' is favoured by political scientists since they
are concerned with interactions across state boundaries, and its use
follows the classic definition of 'going beyond national boundaries or
solely national interests'. While this is a good term in the study of
political inter-relationships it leads to an unfortunate ambiguity in
terms of economics. This arises from its use by Kircher (1964) to mean
ownership of shares in one corporation by nations of several countries.
In his article transnationals result from the merger of large firms in
different nations through exchange of stock, such that ownership of the
firm is pluralistic. Examples are Unilever and Shell, both of which,
have ownership and control split between Dutch and British interests.

Thus 'transnational corporations' are not at all the type of enterprises which operate in Canada or most other nations. If they were,
foreign ownership would not be a problem by definition! Instead, we
have evidence of national concern for sovereignty and independence
due to the dominance of share holding in the foreign (home) nation—
usually the United States. Such US-based, owned, and controlled firms,
which have subsidiaries in foreign nations, such as Canada, where
production takes place in the host nation, are best called multinational
enterprises (MNEs).

This book places heavy emphasis on applications of internalization theory to Canada. Such emphasis reflects both the geographical
location and interest of the author. It seems sensible to include real
world examples of internalization which build upon the author's knowledge rather than upon his lack of experience in other regions. However,
the Canadian examples should be of more than passing interest to the
general reader of the literature on multinationals since Canada is a
representative example of the large number of nations known as small
open economies.

Other nations with similar exposure to the influence of international
trade and investments include Western European nations such as Sweden,
Belgium, the Netherlands and Portugal; Middle Eastern nations such as
Egypt, Iran and Jordan; virtually all African nations including Kenya,

Ghana and Zimbabwe; Australia and New Zealand; and Asian nations such as the Philippines, South Korea and so on. Some of the nations are as developed as Canada; some less developed. All of them have very large international sectors, and in all of them the potential, if not necessarily realized, influence of multinationals is great.

The next two sectors review related work on the topic of internalization undertaken by the author. It is necessary to review these two books in order to place the current work in perspective. One of my previous books applied the theory of internalization to the specific topic of multinationals in Canada. It explored the performance of US multinationals in Canada and criticized the regulation of the MNE. The other book explored the topic of international diversification and reported on empirical studies of the importance of the MNE as a vehicle for international diversification. These two works are now summarized in a little more detail.

Multinationals in Canada — Evaluating their Performance

Economic analysis can be used to evaluate the performance of multinational firms in Canada. In a recent study of US multinationals operating in Canada I tried to find out what they actually do for Canada and how they operate, see Rugman (1980b). Performance is measured by profit rates, after allowing for the effects of transfer pricing, taxation, concentration and other relevant factors that influence the industry within which the multinational enterprise operates.

A major theme is that the multinational enterprise is ultimately an economic creature. It exists to produce and market goods and services from which it can earn profits. I found that it is not the function of the MNE to transfer technology, to act as a development agency or to redistribute income. These are the policy goals of the governments of host nations (such as Canada) in which the MNE operates. While there is clearly some interrelationship between the MNE and government, in my analysis I separated these two powerful actors on the international stage. I assumed that the nation state is not dead but that it has a powerful independent government (or the potential for one) with the power to tax or regulate foreign investment if this is the choice of its electorate.

My approach can be contrasted with those by such political economists as Kari Levitt, Mel Watkins and Abraham Rotstein. These writers tend to mix up efficiency arguments with distributional ones, where the latter are along the lines of regulation and control of foreign investment. It is made clear in my book that restrictions on foreign direct investment will serve only to deny Canada the net economic benefits of higher rates of growth and employment brought to Canada by the MNEs. Instead of controls and regulations, which have led to the establishment of such ineffective and misconceived bodies as the Foreign Investment Review Agency, it is more efficient to use imaginative tax policies to whittle away any excess profits earned by MNEs on their operations in Canada. It is a first-best solution which is based on economic analysis rather than upon the non-economic goals of sovereignty and independence.

My study of the MNE uses a theoretical framework which has been developed only recently. The modern theory of foreign direct investment demonstrates that a US MNE has a firm specific advantage which is exploited in foreign (host) as well as domestic (home) markets. The MNE is, in essence, a response to exogenous market imperfections which can be internalized by the MNE. The new theory of internalization is used extensively in my study and serves as a basis for the analysis of the economic efficiency of MNEs.

Part I of Rugman (1980b) develops the modern theory of the multinational enterprise in a Canadian context, explains the concept of internalization and reviews key theoretical models of foreign investment in order to demonstrate that these theories are in fact sub-cases of the general theory of internalization. It is shown that the multinational enterprise is an efficient vehicle for international production and that its internal market allows it to overcome externalities in the sale of knowledge. Indeed, the multinational firm is able to circumvent most exogenous market imperfections. Concerns about its alleged market power are valid only when it is able to close a market or generate endogenous imperfections. In practice these events rarely occur, unless they are stimulated and fostered as some sort of by-product to a government regulation.

Part II of the study is strictly empirical. It reports data on the profit rates of multinational firms active in Canada, and disaggregates the industry data which have been reported so far, by looking at individual corporations. There are separate sections on multinational firms operating in the resource sector, such as those in minerals and petroleum. Besides the level of profits one chapter also examines the risk of profits of multinational firms. In general, it is found that multinational firms do not earn excessive (above average) profits but they do benefit from a more stable stream of earnings over time than do domestic firms. The latter advantage of multinationals is due to the benefits of international diversification. No evidence is found of transfer pricing in an examination of the performance of MNEs, even when analyzing data on the mining industry.

Part III builds upon the theory and empirical work of earlier sections to criticize existing federal government policy towards foreign direct investment. The reasons for increased Canadian nationalism and the objections to foreign ownership are reviewed. The Foreign Investment Review Agency is judged and found to be in an impossible position as it attempts to satisfy conflicting policy objectives.

A distinction is drawn throughout the work between equity and efficiency objectives. Regulations are an inferior solution to optimal taxes and subsidies as a method for solving distributional goals. Some of the unforeseen tariff and trade implications of the regulation of foreign direct investment in Canada are explored, such that a strong case for the removal of tariff and nontariff barriers to trade is developed. If these were eliminated there would be less foreign direct investment in the first place since US firms could service the Canadian market by exports rather than subsidiary production.

In conclusion, I find that the multinational enterprise is an efficient organization rather than one which exists to exploit nations. It uses its internal market to bypass external imperfections, many of which are natural externalities, such as the lack of a market for knowledge, but some of which (tariffs, taxes and regulations) have been imposed by governments. The multinational enterprise is found to have a net positive economic impact on Canada. There are unresolved problems of equity versus efficiency in any analysis of the multinational enterprise, but this is a problem common to all economic theory. By highlighting this problem in a new context I conclude that more attention must be directed towards the efficiency aspects of multinationals in Canada.

Going Multinational to Reduce Risk

International diversification of investments is a concept whose time has come. Many investors and businessmen have traditionally regarded foreign operations as being more risky than domestic ones, yet in recent years knowledgeable people have become aware of the advantages of international asset holdings. New theoretical developments in the area of finance have been extended into the mainstream of work on international finance. In this work, see Rugman (1979), the mean-variance portfolio theory model and the capital asset pricing model have been applied to demonstrate that it is possible to reduce the risk of any domestic portfolio by going international.

The unique advantage of the resulting international diversification is that it permits the nondiversifiable (or 'systematic risk') of any one stock market, or economy, to be reduced by holding an international portfolio of assets. This unique gain (demonstrated in several recent academic studies) of international diversification is not available from industrial diversification within any one economy. The potential gains are especially important for investors in small open economies.

Yet, to the extent that recent developments in the international monetary system have created barriers to the free movement of capital between nations these potential gains are often denied individual investors. The regulation of capital flows for balance of payments reasons has disguised the opportunities available to investors for international portfolio diversification. Due to such barriers a risk averse individual cannot construct an efficient international portfolio on a private basis. Information costs are too high, taxes vary between nations, and exchange rate risk frequently serves to complicate the calculation of relative advantages from foreign versus domestic investment. But individuals can achieve the benefits of international diversification in an indirect manner.

One solution is to buy shares in a world mutual fund. Such funds have been observed to exhibit more stable returns than purely domestic mutual funds. However, there are institutional barriers to the purchase of shares in truly international trusts, and such funds also suffer from foreign exchange rate risk. Therefore, while the gains from international diversification exist in theory, they are of limited value to the individual risk averter in practice. Empirical studies of international diversification support this finding.

A final avenue for the individual to explore is the purchase of shares in a multinational corporation. Such an international producer is a vehicle for international diversification since it has operations in many nations. Since national economies (like stock markets) are not perfectly positively correlated the foreign operations of a multinational generate more stable streams of both sales and earnings than can be achieved by non-multinationals of similar size.

The reason for the more stable earnings of a multinational is that it is able to stabilize itself on both the demand and supply side. The low correlations between the host nation and economies which purchase its output serve to stabilize multinational sales. Of course, such gains are also open to a firm which is involved in exporting from one base. The extra (special and unique) advantage available to a multinational is through stabilization of its production activities. Its overseas subsidiaries benefit from low correlations'amongst all nations, not just between the host and foreign countries.

In Rugman (1979) both theoretical and empirical work is reported on the financial aspects of multinational corporations to evaluate the benefits of international diversification. An attempt was made to extend the theory of market imperfections, postulated for the goods and factor markets, into the area of imperfections in international financial markets. This market imperfections approach to foreign direct investment is now called the theory of internalization, and is the subject of this book. Internalization theory, in this context, states that financial markets are better integrated than goods markets. In practice, however, it is found that there are barriers to the free movement of international capital. In turn, this implies that there is not a perfect (international) capital market, as would be assumed in finance theory models of domestic stock markets alone. This has an important implication for the type of international diversification pursued – whether by financial or direct foreign investment.

The high (but not perfect) degree of integration of the world's financial markets, as confirmed by my tests of international diversification, using data on world equity market indices, suggests that there are only limited gains to be made from international diversification by financial investment. On the other hand the smaller degree of integration of world goods markets, in which the multinational corporations operate through international production, suggests that there are considerable gains being made by international diversification through direct investment. The performance of multinational firms based in the United States was tested in case studies of petroleum, mining and other sectors, and the performance of subsidiaries operating in Canada was also examined. No evidence of excess profits was found, but significant signs of stable earnings are detected for most multinationals studied. Similar benefits go to multinational banks.

It can be concluded that the multinational corporation is a vehicle for international diversification. Multinationals enjoy stable earnings – a reward for helping to overcome imperfections in the international goods markets. This activity of multinationals serves to make both the goods and financial markets more efficient than they would be otherwise. The extra costs for multinationals of operating abroad are more than offset by the benefits they reap from international diversification

of production, sales and earnings. So if it is not possible to buy shares
of foreign based corporations directly, an alternative investment
strategy is to buy into multinationals.

This book draws upon the theory of the MNE and the studies of its
performance reported in these two earlier works in order to extend
both the theory and empirical analysis of the MNE. It attempts to
produce a synthesis of the previous literature, one in which the theory
of internalization emerges as a general theory of foreign direct investment.
The next chapter develops this point in detail. Later chapters extend the
principle of internalization to other aspects of the performance of the
MNE, such as its financial and technological functions. Policy implications
for the MNE need to be revised in the light of the new theory of internalization.

2 INTERNALIZATION AS A GENERAL THEORY OF FOREIGN DIRECT INVESTMENT*

Introduction[1]

The world is characterized by imperfections in the goods and factor markets which act as barriers to the free trade of goods and services and inhibit private international financial investment. As a result neither factor price equalization nor goods price equalization has been observed. Further, there is a large volume of foreign direct investment and international production by the multinational enterprise (MNE), an activity which cannot be explained readily by conventional trade theory alone.

A large literature has developed in order to offer explanations of the phenomenon of foreign direct investment (FDI) and the reasons for international production by the MNE. It is argued in this study that the existing theories are basically sub-sets of the general theory of internalization. This theory was first advanced by Coase (1937) in a domestic context and by Hymer (1976) in an international dimension. It is synthesized in a book by Buckley and Casson (1976) and in a paper by Dunning (1977). Internalization serves to determine the reasons for the foreign production and sales of the MNE, namely that these activities take place in response to imperfections in the goods and factor market.[2]

The main point of this chapter is its argument that most of the existing literature on the theory of the MNE consists of specific explanations and models developed by individual writers who have spotted one or another of these many imperfections which exist in world markets. For example, several writers have discovered imperfections in the markets for knowledge and information, while others have focused upon imperfections in the capital markets or upon indivisibilities, scale economies and other firm specific externalities. Here these imperfections are identified by the author and are then shown to be different examples of the general theory of internalization.

In this chapter the theory of internalization is explained and then it is applied in a new manner to suggest a possible integration of the theories of FDI advanced by previous writers such as Vernon (1966), Kindleberger (1969), Caves (1971), Aliber (1970), Johnson (1970), Magee (1977a, b), Kojima (1978) and others in recent years. In a related work Dunning (1977) refers to the need for an eclectic approach to the theory of FDI. His approach can be reconciled with the proposition advanced here, namely that internalization provides an integrated theory of FDI by the MNE. For additional surveys of the recent literature on FDI see Dunning (1973), Hufbauer (1975), Rugman (1975), Vernon (1977), Giddy (1978), Hood and Young (1979) and Casson (1979).[3]

Free Trade or the MNE

The first premise of this section is that the theory of FDI is the converse of the pure theory of international trade. If the world were characterized by a model of free trade, there would be no need for the MNE. In a traditional Heckscher-Ohlin model of free trade perfect goods and factor markets are assumed, as are zero transport costs, identical tastes, constant returns to scale and so on. In such a first-best Paretian situation global welfare is maximized by nations producing according to their relative comparative advantage, where this is determined by a difference in factor endowments or some other reason which sets the international price ratio at variance with the domestic price ratio. For evidence of a similar approach see the paper by Niehans and comments on it by Adler in Agmon and Kindleberger (1977).

It can be shown, within the same theoretical framework, that relaxation of some of the assumptions of the trade model, for example, to allow for scale economies or transport costs, still generates gains from trade. Such assumptions must be relaxed sequentially and for each case the rest of the system must be in perfect competition. Then any one of these potential situations is a reason for trade due to a difference between the domestic and foreign price ratios. Yet when the underlying basic conditions of perfect goods and factor markets do not hold, free trade is destroyed and is replaced by second-best solutions such as the MNE.

The modern theory of FDI suggests that the MNE develops in response to imperfections in the goods or factor markets. Then the country specific advantage of a nation – which leads to trade – is replaced by a firm specific advantage internal to an MNE – which leads to FDI. When there is an advantage specific to a firm, such as knowledge or other special information, it can be transported between the home and host nation within the internal market of the MNE. The MNE is a substitute for free trade, in the rigorous terms of economic theory.

If there is an imperfection in the goods market, such as a tariff, then free trade is replaced by the MNE. A tariff imposed by a nation to support its domestic industry will attract the subsidiaries of MNEs, since they can avoid the customs duty by replacing exports with host-nation production. Canada is a prime example of a nation in which protection has led to foreign ownership of most of its manufacturing industry and nearly all of its resources. Presumably the MNEs would not have been attracted into Canada if it had not been for the barriers to trade erected by the Federal government. In a continental economy domestic corporations of either Canada or the USA could sell to an integrated market and such free trade would be efficient.

Imperfections in the factor markets, especially in the market for intermediate goods, always lead to the development of MNEs. The major point of Hymer's seminal thesis of 1960, published in Hymer (1976), is that the MNE has a firm specific advantage, developed in response to one or another market imperfections. He demonstrated that market advantages are achieved if the MNE can acquire factor inputs at a lower cost than its rivals; if it has better distribution and marketing facilities; if it has a monopoly advantage in information, research, knowledge or some other aspect of the production process; or if it makes a differentiated product. Hymer recognized that in these situations the firm can create an internal market to substitute for, or supersede, the regular external market.

To summarize, the MNE is a response to some sort of externality. It overcomes the externality by internalization. If there were perfect goods or factor markets in the first place then there would be no reason for an MNE to develop and free trade would exist. In this theoretical situation we have free trade being determined by country specific factors or a world of market imperfections in which the MNE operates due to firm specific factors. In practice there are elements of both country specific and firm specific factors in existence, so the MNE is more important when there are relatively greater restrictions on free trade than when such barriers are assumed away, as in the Heckscher-Ohlin world.

The Theory of Internalization

Internalization can occur in response to any type of externality in the goods or factor markets. As discussed above, a tariff, or other type of distortion in the goods market, will induce FDI and multinational activity. The essence of internalization theory is the explicit recognition of these worldwide market imperfections which in practice prevent the efficient operation of the international trade and investment. Following this line of thinking it can be argued that the MNE has developed, first, in response to both exogenous government induced regulations and controls (as discussed above) and, secondly, due to other types of market failure (which I call 'natural' externalities). Both types of market failure have destroyed the theoretical reasons for free trade and private foreign investment. The process of internalization permits the management of the MNE to overcome such externalities and governmental regulations in the product market.

The MNE has been an efficient response to natural externalities, that is, market failure in areas of the factor market such as information and knowledge. Imperfections in this factor market, at an international level, tend to generate the MNE. Of particular interest is the lack of regular markets for intermediate products such as research, information and knowledge. These markets cannot be found in international trade because of the risk of loss of the knowledge advantage if direct sales were made in another nation.

Information is an intermediate product *par excellence.* It is the oil which lubricates the engine of the MNE. There is no proper market for the sale of information created by the MNE and therefore no price for it. There are surrogate prices, for example, those found by evaluating the opportunity cost of factor inputs expended in the production and processing of a new research discovery or by an *ex post* evaluation of the extra profits generated by the discovery, assuming all other costs to remain the same. Yet there is no simple interaction of supply and demand to set a market price. Instead the MNE is driven to create an internal market of its own in order to overcome the failure of an external market to emerge for the sale of information. This internal market of the MNE is an efficient response to the given exogenous market imperfection in the determination of the price of information. Internalization allows the MNE to solve the appropriability problem by assigning property rights in knowledge to the MNE organization.

The MNE will organize and administer its internal market for information in the best manner it can, subject to the traditional accounting practices and other conventions which have to be followed. Once an internal market is in place it becomes an integral part of the firm. Then it becomes difficult to distinguish aspects of the firm's organizational structure from its internal pricing. They are now interdependent. The possession of an internal market gives the MNE the ability to produce and distribute goods and services which are intensive in the use of information. It is this ability to utilize effectively information (an intermediate product) on an international level which distinguishes the MNE from other domestic corporations. It explains why the MNE has an advantage in foreign operations, since it can use overseas subsidiaries to produce goods similar to those developed in the home market, where these products all make use of the information monopoly of the MNE.

The creation of an internal market by the MNE permits it to transform an intangible piece of research into a valuable property specific to the firm. The MNE will exploit its advantage in all available markets and will keep the use of information internal to the firm in order to recoup its initial expenditures on research and knowledge generation. Production by subsidiaries is preferable to licensing or joint ventures since the latter two arrangements cannot benefit from the internal market of an MNE. They would therefore dissipate the information monopoly of the MNE, unless foreign markets were segmented by effective international patent laws or other protective devices.

Coase (1937) was the first to recognize 'that the operation of a market costs something' (p. 388) and that the internal organization of a firm can be an efficient method of production. There are transaction, contracting and co-ordinating costs in using the price mechanism which lead frequently to vertical integration within the firm. The four types of costs are: the brokerage cost of finding a correct price; the cost of defining the obligations of parties in a contract; the risk of scheduling and related input costs; and the taxes paid on exchange transactions in a market.

To avoid these costs the management team of the firm (or entrepreneur in the original Coasian conception) can use administrative fiat to set internal (transfer) prices. The firm can then control the production and marketing of an intermediate product through its vertically integrated structure. It is more efficient for the firm to set prices internally only when there are high transactions costs in using a regular market or when such a market cannot exist. It should be noted that the creation of a market by the MNE is not costless, so the MNE is entitled to a fair return for doing internalization.

These fundamental insights of Coase are readily applicable to the MNE. There are presumably more imperfections and greater transactions costs in international than in domestic markets. These give rise to the MNE. It can enjoy worldwide economies of internal organization. These internal advantages must be sufficient to offset the additional costs of operation abroad in unfamiliar political and economic environments in order to have FDI replace potential indigenous production. Once established abroad the MNE will then use its internal organization to defend its market advantage. This advantage may have been generated, for example, in the firm specific use of knowledge, information, management or marketing skills. Furthermore, the process of internalization by the MNE is a dynamic one. The MNE attempts to prevent dissipation of its knowledge (or other type of) advantage by maintaining control over the production and sales of final products which incorporate this firm specific advantage. Frequently, FDI is preferable to licensing since the latter process involves the risk of dissipation of the knowledge advantage. These points are explored in greater detail in Giddy and Rugman (1979).

The genesis of the concept of internalization can be traced back to Hymer's dissertation of 1960, published as Hymer (1976). As discussed above, he identified at least four types of market imperfections which generate the MNE. His theoretical conception was used by Kindleberger (1969) to build up a modern theory of FDI based on product and factor market imperfections, scale economies and government regulations, taxes and tariffs. These all serve to induce FDI by the MNE rather than portfolio investment or exporting. While these authors make market imperfections the centre of their theory, neither specifically identifies internalization as a paradigm for the theory of FDI.

The first explicit treatment of the relationship between knowledge market imperfections and internalization of markets for intermediate goods is in Buckley and Casson (1976). There is also an excellent synthesis of the modern literature of FDI, built around the concept of internalization, in Dunning (1977). The classic work of Buckley and Casson is reviewed in Giddy (1978) and summarized very ably in Hood and Young (1979). The most rigorous treatment of internalization yet has appeared in Casson (1979).

Others to recognize the applicability of the Coasian model of the firm to the MNE are McManus (1972) and Brown (1976). Unfortunately their contributions have been largely ignored by other economists and they had no impact on the separate development of internalization as a paradigm for FDI by economists associated with the University of Reading, such as Dunning, Casson, Buckley and, to some extent, Hood and Young (1979), Hirsch (1976) and others.

Of course, it is not too surprising that economists in different locations should recognize almost simultaneously the relevance of the Coasian Theorem, since in the early 1970s there was greater public discussion and theoretical analysis of the role of the MNE than in any previous time period. It would be natural for a well-trained economist to focus upon one or another of the market imperfections affecting the MNE. With the benefit of hindsight we can now see that it is a short step to move from analysis of one particular imperfection towards the development of a general theory of FDI, in which all of the reasons for market failures are related to the internal organization of the MNE.

Internalization as a General Theory

It has now been shown that internalization is a refinement of the market imperfections approach and that it explains why the MNE has a firm specific rather than a country specific advantage. Internalization is a synthesizing explanation of the motives for FDI. To demonstrate that the existing theories of FDI are really sub-cases of the theory of internalization it is now necessary to examine the more important versions of some of the important but apparently different models of FDI.

One of the most influential treatments of externalities and market imperfections is in Caves (1971). He is able to link the imperfect market for knowledge with arguments which suggest that the MNE will respond to such an imperfection by engaging in product differentiation and horizontal integration, the latter to extend its monopoly advantage into world markets. The MNE tends to operate in oligopolistic markets and these encourage it to differentiate its product, or to utilize scale economies or some other firm specific advantage. The 'Caves economies' of product differentiation advantages and horizontal integration can be contrasted with the 'Coase economies' of information and knowledge advantages which occur under vertical integration. Both types are stressed here since they are the essence of internalization. The MNE is usually both vertically and horizontally integrated, so it is able to maintain its firm specific advantage quite readily.

Other writers have focused upon the imperfect nature of the knowledge advantage of the MNE, without relating this explicitly to internalization. Johnson (1970) has shown that knowledge is a public good with a zero social price but a non-zero private cost which is borne by corporations as they engage in research and development. To substitute for the missing regular market for knowledge production the MNE can create an internal market of its own in which the use of information by foreign subsidiaries can be monitored and repaid by fees payable to the parent firm (or other knowledge generator).

Magee (1977a, b) extends Johnson's analysis to deal with the appropriability problem of new information and technology for which there is no regular market. These ideas are synthesized in Casson (1979) who demonstrates, in perhaps the most rigorous explanation of internalization to date, that the use of an internal market permits the MNE to retain control over its advantage in proprietary information. Production by subsidiaries is preferable to licensing since the latter method involves a probable loss of control of the information monopoly obtained only at considerable expense by the MNE. Internalization allows the MNE to appropriate a fair return for its costly knowledge expenditures.

In an interesting paper, Hirsch (1976) has developed a model of international trade and production. In it he explores the conditions required for exporting or FDI by a firm endowed with a firm specific knowledge advantage, K. Although not stated explicitly, his model treats K as an intermediate product which is internalized in the structure of the MNE. Hirsch unfortunately does not consider explicitly the conditions for licensing, the third possible method of servicing a foreign market, along with exporting or FDI. This third option, of licensing, is viable at the end of the firm's technology cycle rather than at an early stage of foreign activity as is sometimes argued in the literature on international business. Hirsch also largely ignores the dynamic nature of technology, that is, the changing conditions under which the MNE can appropriate its firm specific advantage in K.

In his classic statement of the product cycle model Vernon (1966) offers a powerful generalization of the process of FDI. As is well known, he identifies three stages of product development and uses these to explain the cross-over of exports and imports for three types of nations, over time. Initially the new product is produced by the home nation (often the USA) and exported to other nations. Next, as the product matures it starts to be produced by other (advanced) nations, often by subsidiaries of the home nation's MNEs. Finally the good becomes a standardized product, i.e., one when no monopoly in information or other firm specific advantage is retained. In this third stage production can start up in less developed nations, continue in other advanced nations, but will decline in the home nation so that it now imports a product which was once exported.

The relevance of the internalization theory to Vernon's product cycle model lies in the basic motivation of research and knowledge generation which promotes a new product. The appropriate questions to ask are: what generates the initial research discovery in the home nation, and how can there be successive waves of product cycles once such research discoveries continue on a dynamic basis? Clearly the dynamic nature of research generation lies at the heart of the theory of internalization, so the product cycle model is a sub-case of it. Once the motivation of research is explained by internalization then everything else in the product cycle model follows.

Similarly in his latest work Vernon (1977) is concerned about the spectre of entropy facing MNEs. The MNE is in one of several categories, that is, in an innovation-based oligopolistic framework, or in a mature oligopoly or a senescent oligopoly. Vernon argues that the firm specific advantage of an MNE is in constant danger of being eroded and that the firm needs to overcome entropy to generate new advantages. Again the basic motivation factor for FDI can be seen to be the need for an MNE to generate firm specific advantages in a dynamic manner — the essence of internalization. Giddy (1978) has recognized this in a paper which relates the product cycle model to the theory of internalization.

Defensive FDI is often undertaken by MNEs in an oligopolistic industry. They are concerned with protecting their market shares on a worldwide basis as well as on a domestic one. The concept of defensive investment was first postulated by Alexandre Lamfalussy (1961) for domestic investment and has been applied in an international context, where it has received its most detailed treatment, by Knickerbocker (1973). The latter author found that foreign subsidiaries of firms in an oligopolistic industry tended to be established in clusters, that is once one MNE set up a subsidiary in a nation then its rivals responded by opening their own affiliates in that market. Using an entry concentration index for each industry, Knickerbocker found that half of the two thousand US foreign subsidiaries established between 1948 and 1967 were formed in three-year industry clusters and that three quarters of the total were formed in at least seven year clusters. He used data from the Harvard multinational data bank for the 187 US multinationals identified by the project to confirm the oligopolistic reaction hypothesis.

The theory of defensive FDI and oligopolistic reaction by the MNEs is explained by the general theory of internalization. In the first place there must exist an initial imperfect market, such as an oligopoly with price leadership or some collusion, in order to generate the concern with market shares on a world basis. If this oligopoly structure exists in a domestic industry and a firm engages in FDI to secure its share of a foreign market then it is clearly attempting to retain its firm specific advantage, as will any MNE. Therefore, the theory of oligopolistic reaction is yet another example of firm specific advantages being exploited through FDI. Secondly, what the theory fails to explain is the reason for an initial foreign investment decision by one of the members of the oligopoly, to which the other members react. This initial FDI is explained by some other theory such as the product cycle model in which one firm generates a technological advantage, or by an attempt of the firm to differentiate its product and segment markets. In short, many of the reasons for the motivation of FDI can be applied here as explanations of the initial foreign investment. Since these reasons for FDI have already been shown to be part of internalization theory then the oligopolistic reaction hypothesis is another sub-case of internalization.

Kojima (1978) has proposed a 'Japanese model' of FDI which is trade biased, i.e., one in which FDI in resources, or other sectors where Japan has a comparative disadvantage, acts as a complement to trade. He used a modified Heckscher-Ohlin model in which management skills and knowledge appear as a factor input – a specific factor model. Kojima argues that American FDI is trade destroying since it typically occurs in sectors where the United States has a large comparative advantage. Here FDI substitutes for trade, serves to export employment abroad and results in balance of payments problems. Kojima is extremely critical of the product cycle model and its variants which he terms the 'American model' of FDI, since this model acts as an apologia for the transfer abroad of those industries in which the United States has a comparative advantage – due to its technological superiority.

The main problem with Kojima's analysis is that it is set in the static framework of trade theory. His model needs perfect markets and the assumptions of a Heckscher-Ohlin world. Clearly it is a mistake to regard technology as a homogeneous product over time and to ignore the dynamic nature of the technology cycle. It is probable that the United States has a comparative advantage, not in technology itself but in the generation of new knowledge. Therefore it is feasible for US FDI in technology to take place to secure new markets on a continuous basis, as successive stages of the technology cycle are exploited, first in domestic markets and then in foreign ones.

Contrary to Kojima's allegations most American FDI is not trade destroying but, in general, is undertaken to replace free trade. There are major barriers to trade in technologically advanced goods, due both to exogenous government imposed controls and also to endogenous restrictions imposed by the MNE. The latter restrictions are necessary since knowledge is a public good and only through the process of internalization is it feasible for a firm to organize a market for new technology. The MNE will seek out foreign markets in which price discrimination can be practised in order to maximize its return on the information monopoly internal to the firm. Control over the use of information is necessary for the MNE to appropriate a private return for its investment in knowledge creation. FDI is a superior device to licensing since production and marketing by subsidiaries allow the MNE better to avoid the risk of dissemination of its technological knowledge. FDI also replaces exporting once the latter is denied by tariffs, controls and other government imposed barriers to free trade. Thus FDI is trade replacing rather than trade destroying.

The location economics approach to FDI can also be regarded as an aspect of internalization, this time in a spatial context. The MNE can save transport costs by setting up an overseas subsidiary rather than relying on exports from the home nation. This spatial cost saving is another example of a firm specific advantage internalized by the MNE. As Robock *et al.* (1977) demonstrate (in Chapter 3) the location economies are more important for market-oriented MNEs than for ones in the aircraft or heavy engineering industries, since the latter types of product can achieve only a limited saving in transport costs.

The location economics approach fails to recognize that international production is done by the MNE, so a firm specific explanation of the reasons for international activity is required. This is that most MNEs are attempting to produce, and market, differentiated products; or they are creating an internal market for an intermediate good. In these cases the spatial dimension of MNE activity complements the other firm specific advantages characteristic of multinationals.

Location theory is not an independent explanation of FDI but one which serves to reinforce the powerful predictive nature of internalization theory. Within the MNE knowledge is internationally mobile, transported by its internal market. While the sourcing of production by the MNE to service its foreign markets is often determined by location economics, the overall structure and operations of the MNE are determined by firm specific advantages. Ultimately, the MNE is always a creature of internalization.

In a slightly different context Leff (1978) has hypothesized that the imperfect goods and factor markets of poorer nations can be somewhat overcome by the 'group' form of industrial organization. The group is a multicompany firm run by owners and/or managers from a common cultural background and is frequently an association of individuals or families who are wealthy relative to their neighbours. The group performs as an intermediary in pooling risks and in reducing information costs. It appears, therefore, to be a primitive type of Coasian firm searching for the benefits of an internal market. It is not clear if Leff firms are purely domestic ones, or if they have international activities. If they are not MNEs then the potential benefits of internalization are limited to the gains from avoiding market imperfections within the domestic economy. Clearly there are greater gains to be made on an international scale, given the lack of perfect integration of the economic and financial markets of poorer and richer nations.

Aliber (1970) makes an interesting attempt to introduce foreign exchange risk into the theory of FDI. He assumes a world with different currency areas in which an MNE is able to borrow funds more cheaply than potential competitors in host nations since there is a premium on the currency of the home nation. This enhances the income stream of the MNE and permits it to engage in risky investments in the host nations. In effect the MNE has a lower cost of capital due to its lower perceived foreign exchange rate risk.

Aliber's model was postulated at a time when there was a premium on the US dollar and it appeared to explain the relatively large FDI by US-based MNEs fairly well. Further, the model helps to explain recent developments such as the rapid growth of European and Japanese based MNEs, given the changeover to a premium on their currencies compared to the US dollar. However, the model does not explain the continued net outflow of FDI from America in recent years, albeit at a reduced rate compared to the 1960s.

In any event Aliber's model can be interpreted as another example of a firm specific advantage being internalized by the MNE. Here the advantage is in borrowing local funds in the host nation, given a strong home nation currency. The MNE enjoys this advantage in raising capital due to its internal structure which transcends national capital markets and permits it to calculate the risk and return of alternative investment in a broader manner than is possible for a uninational firm.

The theory of internalization can also be applied to the area of international diversification. The recent literature on international diversification has demonstrated a superior stock market performance for MNEs compared to uninational firms, after allowing for size and industry differences—see Rugman (1977a, b and 1979). This superior performance is due to the advantage of the MNE in its exploitation of information through an internal market. The role of the MNE as a surrogate vehicle for individual international diversification in a world of capital market imperfections is intimately related to its ability to create an internal market which bypasses such imperfections. Here, as in the areas of imperfect markets discussed before, the MNE is responding in an efficient manner to an exogenous market imperfection.

International diversification has been a very useful addition to the literature on the MNE, since it directs attention towards the risk (variability) of earnings as well as their level (and most other theories ultimately show how the profit rate of the MNE is affected by the relevant market imperfection). Clearly the MNE only needs to be regarded as an indirect vehicle for international diversification when individual investors are confronted with financial market imperfections which make it impossible for them to build up efficient world portfolios themselves. Therefore the imperfections in the world's capital markets (or, at least, their lack of perfect integration) is another example of market failure leading to internalization (this time financial, rather than real) by the MNE. These points are discussed in more detail in Rugman (1979).

If a more interdisciplinary view is taken, the relevance of internalization as a central theory is retained. For example, much of the work by behavioural scientists focuses upon the strategy and structure of management decision making within the MNE – a clear emphasis upon the internal market activity of the MNE. Similarly, research by those in marketing and management science frequently seeks to evaluate the success of the global planning of the MNE or examines various other aspects of the organization and operation of the MNE's internal market. Some of these issues are examined by a group of behavioural scientists and economists in a new book edited by Negandhi (1980). It will probably be some time before a truly interdisciplinary approach to the MNE can be worked out but at least internalization is a promising route to follow.

Conclusion and Implications

The theory of internalization explains that the MNE develops an internal market in response to an externality. In the case of a classic externality – the failure of the market mechanism to set a price for the private production and dissemination of knowledge – the internal market of the MNE allows proprietary information to be used efficiently. The MNE can overcome an exogenous market imperfection governing the production of knowledge or another intermediate good by internalizing this externality. In a similar vein the concept of internalization can be applied to other areas of market imperfection, including those in international good, labour and capital markets. The same implication is reached, namely that the MNE is a device for the formation and exploitation of internal markets.

One of the problems in modelling the MNE is that it has the power, on occasions, to endogenize an imperfection and perpetuate a firm specific advantage. This is inefficient. Yet most market imperfections that exist in the real world are truly exogenous or are erected by governments. It is the latter imperfections, such as tariffs, taxes and controls on international capital, that are of particular relevance in explaining the rise of the MNE. While the formation of the internal market is usually in response to a market imperfection the continued exploitation of the firm specific advantage by the MNE often serves to maintain the advantage in an endogenous manner. Thus the MNE is both a victim of external market imperfections and a villain in seeking to retain them.

The process of internalization explains most (and probably all) of the reasons for FDI. Previous writers in the literature on the motives for FDI have tended to identify one or more of the imperfections in factor or product markets, or have noticed a response by the MNE to government induced market imperfections such as tariffs, taxes and capital controls. All of these types of market imperfection serve to stimulate one sort of MNE or another. The MNE is in the business of internalizing externalities. It is now time to recognize that internalization is a general theory of FDI and a unifying paradigm for the theory of the MNE.

Notes

* This chapter first appeared in *Weltwirtschaftliches Archiv* (*Review of World Economics*), vol. 116, no. 2 (Tubingen: J.C.B. Mohr, June 1980): 365-79. Reprinted with permission.

1. Helpful comments on a previous version of this chapter, first presented to the annual meeting of the Eastern Economic Association at Boston in April 1979 were made by Winston Brown at the conference and, on other occasions, by Mark Casson, John Dunning, Ian Giddy, Stefan Robock and Raymond Vernon. Additional comments were made by participants at seminars at Columbia University, Concordia University and Dalhousie University.

2. The concept of internalization has been developed by economists associated with the University of Reading in England. A clear statement of the benefits and costs of internalization appears in Buckley and Casson (1976), especially in Chapter 2. A more extensive and rigorous theoretical treatment is in Casson (1979), especially Chapters 2 and 3. The work of John Dunning has always sought to integrate the theories of FDI and it is instructive to contrast his comprehensive survey of the field in Dunning (1973), in which internalization is not mentioned, with his major unifying synthesis in Dunning (1977) where it is the central concept. Many of the ideas expressed in this paper originate from either the written work of Casson and Dunning, or from conversations that I have enjoyed with them.

3. Two recent textbooks in international economics also contain good surveys of the pre-internalization literature on FDI. These are the ones by Herbert G. Grubel

(1977a) and H. Peter Gray (1979). Unfortunately most writers in international economics and international business have either neglected the theory of the MNE as a separate topic, despite the great importance of MNEs in trade and exchange, or (at best) have incorporated it as a section in long-term capital flows, whereas it belongs on its own with its distinctive theoretical rationale, namely internalization.

3 THE CHOICE BETWEEN TRADE, FOREIGN DIRECT INVESTMENT AND LICENSING

Introduction

This chapter examines the choice between exporting, foreign direct investment and licensing as methods of servicing foreign markets. The choice is made by a multinational enterprise (MNE), assumed to possess a firm specific advantage in knowledge, technology or some other special asset embodied within the organization of the firm. Alternative methods of determination of the optimal modality are presented. This form of presentation is used here since there are as yet unresolved problems in the solution of some of these models. It is advisable to provide as much information as possible so that a definitive model may emerge later from these pioneering attempts at formalizing the cost conditions affecting each modality.

The choice between exporting and foreign direct investment (FDI) has been discussed in previous work by Horst (1973, 1974) and Hirsch (1976). This section proceeds in the spirit of these authors to consider the conditions favouring exporting, direct investment, and a third alternative, licensing. The point is also made explicit that the MNE is a monopolist. It is assumed to have a firm specific advantage in knowledge (broadly defined to include technological and/or managerial skills). This advantage is retained within the organizational structure of the MNE. The monopolistic nature of the firm specific advantage leads to excess profits (or 'rents') but these are reduced by the special costs of alternative modes of servicing the foreign markets in which the MNE operates. These special costs are inherent in running an internal market, so the excess profits of the MNE are always less than they would be if a regular market were available.

In the discussion of the relative choices to be made by the MNE between the three options it is recognized that the firm runs the risk of dissipation of its firm specific advantage if it engages in licensing, since the licensee may be able to resell information about the firm specific advantage of the MNE to outside parties. Previous writers such as Magee (1977a, b), Buckley and Casson (1976) and Casson (1979) have identified this as the appropriability problem. This problem is common to all innovation or knowledge production. Here use is made of the economics of information and public goods to identify the specific

53

conditions under which the MNE switches from one mode of market servicing to another. Also discussed are the potential repercussions for future sales by the multinational firm once licensing is undertaken in a world which does not have perfectly segmented markets for knowledge. This model is a useful extension of the literature, since it builds upon the potentially unifying paradigm of internalization and adds some analytical insight into the complex decisions facing the MNE.

The Hirsch Method Extended

The first method of choosing between the three modes adapts and modifies substantially the model of Hirsch (1976), updated in Agmon and Hirsch (1979). The variables, as defined below, are specified in present value terms. All the variables are either normal costs of the production function, or special costs associated with one of the three modalities as the MNE chooses the best alternative. This presentation extends the original Hirsch model to licensing and replaces his concept of knowledge (K) as a sunk cost to a potential rival firm by treating the risk of dissipation of the firm specific advantage from the viewpoint of the MNE, since this is the firm making the investment decision. The first three cases present the choice of mode for the MNE to service a foreign market. Later the conditions for servicing the home market are considered. At this stage constant levels of investment and risk are assumed.

The notation used is as follows:

C   Normal costs of producing the good in the home country.
C*   Normal costs of producing the good in the foreign (*) host country.
M*   Export marketing costs, including insurance, transport and tariffs (later M* are defined as information costs only).
A*   Additional costs to foreign firms operating in the foreign country, especially environmental, cultural and political information costs.
D*   Knowledge dissipation costs associated with the risk of compromising the firm specific advantage once a licence is granted. These costs are borne by the MNE but are lower in segmented factor markets.

Using this notation it is possible to state the following relationships for the three modes of servicing a foreign market:

(i)　Export if: $C + M^* < C^* + A^*$
　　　　　　　(exporting is cheaper than FDI)
　　　　　and $C + M^* < C^* + D^*$
　　　　　　　(exporting is cheaper than licensing)
(ii)　FDI if:　$C^* + A^* < C + M^*$
　　　　　　　(FDI is cheaper than exporting)
　　　　　and $C^* + A^* < C^* + D^*$
　　　　　　　(FDI is cheaper than licensing)
(iii)　License if: $C^* + D^* < C^* + A^*$
　　　　　　　(licensing costs less than FDI)
　　　　　and $C^* + D^* < C + M^*$
　　　　　　　(licensing costs less than exporting)

The MNE will choose the mode for servicing a foreign market according to these conditions, all other things assumed constant. This assumption of *ceteris paribus* is crucial since without it the variables would be influenced by different determinants and would not be independent. These choices will be optimal only if the MNE has full information on each of the special costs, which are the only relevant variables in making the decision. Then it is necessary to develop a theory about the way in which the special costs change in relation to each other over time. But first some special cases are developed as extensions of this approach.

The work thus far, and other studies in the same vein, have assumed that the multinational enterprise is focusing on the choice of entry mode for a foreign market. Yet direct investment abroad, or licensing, can occur in order to service not the local host market but that of the home country, or even a third market. Then the choice of production location and ownership strategy can be analyzed in a fashion similar to the procedure so far. To illustrate consider the special cases of offshore production and licensing for the domestic market. When will they occur?

Assume the multinational firm is a 'global scanner' and wishes to identify the most profitable means of exploiting its monopolistic advantage in its home market. It has three choices:

(a)　produce at home,
(b)　produce abroad for the domestic market,
(c)　license a foreign firm to produce for export to the domestic market.

The profitability of each of these methods is simply sales revenues minus production costs, less any special costs associated with international business. Since the revenues can be assumed given, the choice among the three depends on relative production costs in the two countries (location specific factors), and on the special 'multinational firm' costs (firm specific factors). Thus the following situations emerge:

(a) the cost of producing at home is C.

(b) the cost of producing abroad for import to the home market is $C^* + M + A^*$, where M is the additional marketing cost associated with importing (such as tariffs), and A^* is the additional cost of being a foreign investor in the host country.

(c) the cost of licensing a foreign firm for import is $C^* + M + D^*$, where D^* is, as before, the risk of lost profits from dissipation of the licensed knowledge.

From these can be derived the conditions for each mode of servicing the domestic market. They are:

(i) produce at home if: $C < C^* + M + A^*$
$$\text{and } C < C^* + M + D^*$$

(ii) offshore assembly produce abroad for import if:
$$C^* + M + A^* < C$$
$$\text{and } C^* + M + A^* < C^* + M + D^*$$

(iii) trading licensee allow production by a licensee if:
$$C^* + M + D^* < C^* + M + A^*$$
$$\text{and } C^* + M + D^* < C$$

These conditions are directly analogous to those associated with entering a foreign market, except that since the multinational firm itself is presumably the seller in its domestic market, it can obtain the monopolistic profits from sales to that market directly. This means it need not charge a royalty to the foreign licensee for the use of its special advantage; competition among potential licensees will ensure that the licensee's price is kept to the competitive minimum. The price and sales volume are necessarily established by the licensor as part of the agreement.

The choice of mode of servicing a domestic market can be expressed in terms of demand and cost conditions, the relative values of which change over time. The optimal mode of servicing thus changes over time too. The analysis of these changes will be similar to the analysis of the evolving choice of entry method for a foreign market. The next section extends the methodology introduced here by considering the special costs of each mode in more detail. It develops a model in which the relative changes in the special costs with respect to time permit the MNE to choose between the optimal mode over time.

The Net Present Value Method

Another method of choosing between the three modalities can make use of a net present value (NPV) approach. This approach is not fully worked out here but is included to illustrate the nature of the method. The potential advantage of the NPV approach is that it captures some quasi-dynamic elements of the choice of optimal mode. The MNE should, in principle, calculate the NPV of each of the three modalities by considering the difference between the discounted revenues and costs (both normal and special). It should then choose the mode which has the maximum NPV for the length of time it is anticipated that the market will be serviced. It is likely that the optimal NPV may change over time, and the MNE should attempt to identify the basic switch-over points between modes, although this NPV method cannot itself distinguish such a sequence of entry modes. There is a once and for all choice of entry mode at a specific time.

Clearly the specification of a comprehensive model which incorporates interdependencies between the revenues and costs over time, considers possible reversals in the dynamic NPV choice path and deals with other theoretical problems is a major task. Here these issues are simplified by making the assumption of certainty in information. Then the choice of mode by the MNE is less affected by interdependencies, sequential decision making and feedback effects. The MNE makes a once and for all choice of mode at the outset of the model by calculating the NPV of each mode, given all the available information at that time. The MNE picks the optimal sequence of modes, and then switches between them, such that NPV is maximized at each point on its finite time horizon.

The notation is as before:

R   Total revenues from sales of the final product which uses the firm specific advantage in knowledge as an intermediate good.

C   Total costs of labour, capital and other normal inputs in the home nation.

C*   Total costs of labour, capital and other normal inputs in the foreign nation.

M*   Export marketing costs, i.e. information costs about the foreign nation.

A*   Additional costs of servicing a foreign market by FDI.

D*   Costs of dissipation of the firm specific advantage.

All variables are specified for a time period, t. The initial date of entry into a foreign market is defined as te, which may, or may not, be time zero.

There are again three options open to a firm in servicing a foreign market. The firm can export (E), use foreign direct investment (FDI), or license the knowledge advantage (L). The net present value (NPV) of each of these three options is shown as follows:

$$\text{Exporting: } NPV_E = \sum_{t=te}^{t} \frac{R_t - C_t - M_t^*}{(1 + r)^t}$$

$$\text{FDI: } NPV_{FDI} = \sum_{t=te}^{t} \frac{R_t - C_t^* - A_t^*}{(1 + r)^t}$$

$$\text{Licensing: } NPV_L = \sum_{t=te}^{t} \frac{R_t - C_t^* - D_t^*}{(1 + r)^t}$$

It is assumed that the special costs, M*, A* and D* all fall over time.

To determine the relative value to a firm in servicing foreign markets, it is necessary to consider the net present value (NPV) of each of the three options. The conditions are:

(1)   Export when $NPV_E > \max(NPV_{FDI'}\ NPV_L)$.

(2)   FDI when $NPV_{FDI} > \max(NPV_{E'}\ NPV_L)$.

(3)   License when $NPV_L > \max(NPV_{E'}\ NPV_{FDI})$.

It is hypothesized that M* is less than A* since the former special costs involves information about the foreign goods market only, while A* involves gaining information about the foreign factor market in addition to the goods market. This follows from the special property of FDI, namely that it involves foreign production (as well as marketing). The MNE thus faces information costs of the foreign labour and capital markets, and their associated political and financial environments. These additional costs of the factor market are not required under the export marketing mode. Although A* can be avoided by licensing, this third mode is hypothesized to have the greatest special cost, since there is a grave risk of dissipation of the firm specific advantage of the MNE by premature, or inappropriately priced, licensing. Most MNEs with genuine firm specific advantages to safeguard will not want to put their very monopoly position at risk. So D* is assumed greater than A* (and therefore M*).

It is apparent that the most interesting variables in these equations are the special costs associated with each mode of entry. Otherwise the normal costs of production, C or C*, and the revenues R are assumed constant for each alternative. For the valuation of each modality to change it is necessary to have a theory about the relative values of the special costs M*, A* and D*. As explained above it is hypothesized that:

$$M^* < A^* < D^*$$

This leads to three equations for the special costs:

$$M_t^* = a + bt^c$$

$$A_t^* = e + ft^g$$

$$D_t^* = h + qt^p$$

The key hypothesis of the model sets the sign restrictions on the exponents as:

$$c < g < p$$

It is also assumed that the fixed costs start highest for D* and are lowest for M*, so:

$$a < e < h$$

Given these conditions if the MNE were to follow a cost minimizing strategy it would be confined to a pattern of first exporting, then FDI and finally licensing. This strategic choice of entry mode is identical to maximization under the NPV method, since the variables specified have the same properties. The model can be extended by relaxing some of these assumptions, for example over time demand conditions may vary and affect the choice of mode. These extensions are left for future work.

In conclusion this section presented a model of the multinational firm operating in two or more countries. An internally-generated, monopolistically-held knowledge-like advantage was produced in the home country and exploited abroad by means of exporting, foreign direct investment or licensing. The model was used to derive the conditions under which each mode of entry is selected, and hence the likely choice of mode of entry.

This model is one in which the multinational enterprise seeks to maximize the net present value of its monopolistically-held advantage in a particular foreign market. It can itself produce at home or abroad for direct sale to the foreign market; but when it does so, it faces additional distance costs, which diminish with the MNE's experience in the country. These costs are not borne by a host-country firm, potentially a rival producer of the same product. On the other hand it would be very expensive for the foreign firm to develop for itself the MNE's advantage. Normally, therefore, foreign firms begin production only when it is to both firms' advantage for the MNE to sell or license its advantage to the foreign firm.

In the real world, revenues, normal production costs and special international business costs, all change with time. The net profit from any one mode of entry, however, changes at a rate different from that of the others; hence at some point it pays the MNE to switch modes. Since this is a certainty model, the firm can predict in advance which entry method will be the most profitable and when. In choosing potential switchover times, therefore, it will choose the sequence of modes that will maximize the net present value of all future cash flows. The choice depends upon the length of time it is anticipated that the market will be serviced. Given the conditions assumed here ($M^* < A^* < D^*$) this sequence of entry mode is most likely to be exporting, followed later by FDI and ultimately by licensing. The next section explores these conditions using a simple diagram for choice of mode.

Firm Specific (Monopoly) Advantages and Entry Method

The key characteristic of the MNE is that it has a firm specific advantage in knowledge. Therefore, by definition, the MNE is a monopolist. Naturally there are potential competitors and seekers of the knowledge of the MNE, but as long as the MNE retains control over its firm specific advantage all is well. To retain control over the use of its monopolistic advantage the MNE is compelled to favour use of an internal market. Contractual arrangements, such as licensing and joint ventures, are fraught with danger for the MNE. An inappropriate form of non-equity involvement has the potential to destroy the firm specific advantage of the MNE, without which it ceases to be a monopolist and runs the risk of fading away into nothing.

This section examines the monopolistic nature of the firm specific advantage of the MNE, and the implications of this monopoly characteristic. Using the symbols outlined previously, Figure 3.1 is now developed. Based on the assumption of a firm specific advantage, the average revenue (demand) curve of the MNE is drawn as downward sloping. Every MNE has an incentive to keep some slope on its curve, that is, to engage in product differentiation or some other activity which generates a monopoly characteristic.

In this section a model of the MNE is developed to demonstrate the profit maximizing conditions for entry into a foreign market. The MNE is assumed to have a firm specific advantage in knowledge and can choose between the three modes of exporting, foreign direct investment and licensing. Special costs are unique to each of these modes and these are seen to determine the choice made by the MNE. The characteristic of the model in this chapter is the classification of costs facing the MNE as it considers how to service the foreign market, or markets. There are two classifications of costs.

First, there are normal costs of production: C for the home nation, and C* for the foreign nation(s). These normal costs are best thought of as aggregate production functions with information in them about the costs of labour, capital, resources, technology and other inputs of the respective nations. In short, they capture the country specific factors of the nations. Thus they include all normal considerations that determine a nation's comparative advantage. The MNE has to take these costs as exogenous.

Secondly, there are special costs of production: M*, A* and D*. These costs capture the unique costs of each mode as the MNE involves itself in one or another of the modes of entry to foreign markets. The special costs need to be distinguished from the normal country specific (exogenous) costs of producing at home or abroad. The special costs are endogenous to the MNE and are therefore the primary determinants of its choice of mode.

The firm specific factor is not shown as a cost but is best thought of as an asset embodied in the MNE. Thus the firm specific factor is reflected in the revenues available to the MNE and assumed constant for each mode. The closest the firm specific advantage comes to being included as a cost is in the licensing mode, as discussed below.

The special costs are fixed in each time period and can be modelled as if they are equivalent to lump-sum taxes. The special costs do not vary with output and hence do not affect the firm's marginal cost curves. Nor can they be shifted onto consumers by the MNE, so each special cost serves to reduce the excess profits of the firm in a unique manner. The special costs are allowed to vary over time at different rates. This generates three separate time paths of special costs, one for each mode of servicing a foreign market. The MNE finds the optimal mode of production by setting marginal costs (normal plus appropriate special cost) equal to marginal revenue at the start of each time period. The MNE finds the mode that maximizes profits (π) in each period. Its choice depends crucially upon the relative amount of each special cost, M^*, A^* or D^*, which are now defined in more detail.

M^* are the additional costs of export marketing which arise from gathering information about a foreign country and its potential market. These costs are initially high but diminish over time as familiarity with the new market increases. There are also other export marketing costs, invariant with time, arising from transportation, insurance, tariffs and other barriers to international trade. This model does not explore these other costs, which are likely to vary with output and therefore can be incorporated into the marginal cost curve of the firm. These costs are added to C, the normal cost of production in the home nation.

A^* are defined as additional information costs of foreign direct investment arising from the unfamiliarity of the MNE with the culture, politics and economy of the host nation. These costs are separate from C^*, the normal costs of production in the foreign (host) nation.

D^* can be viewed in general as the potential loss associated with the risk of attempting to separate the firm's special advantage from the firm itself. If the advantage is a brand name, some sales may be lost. If, as in the present context, the advantage is knowledge, the cost equals the profits lost because of dissipation of knowledge. These risks of dissipation costs are added to C^*, the normal cost of production in the foreign nation.

The profitability of each of the modalities depends crucially upon the relative value of each of the special costs, and is best illustrated in Figure 3.1.

In Figure 3.1 the linear demand function, AR, represents demand for the final good at various prices in the foreign nation. For the exporting mode MC is the marginal cost or supply function for exports from the home country. Since product differentiation and control over the inter-mediate product (knowledge) provides the firm with at least a temporary monopoly in the sale of the good, quantity (Q^*) is set where marginal revenue equals marginal cost, and price (P^*) is found at the corresponding point on the AR function.

In Figure 3.1 the total profit from exporting is given by the area P^*ZX^1X, which represents total revenue OP^*ZQ^* minus total costs $OVYQ^*$ and the special export marketing costs, represented by area XX^1YV. The size of the one-period profit is a function of the position and slope of the demand function AR, the position and slope of the normal supply function MC, and the special costs associated with the entry mode. Since the host-country demand curve is unaffected by the mode of entry, the chief factors in considering the exporting alternative will be the relative production costs of producing in the two countries, and the additional marketing costs, M^*.

The second entry method is foreign direct investment. Its distinguish-ing features are that it involves production within the foreign country by a subsidiary which is under the direct managerial control of the multinational firm. This has two implications. The first is that the multinational faces certain additional costs (A^*) not encountered by local host-country firms. The second implication is that retaining ownership and control of production enables the firm to forestall dissipation of its special advantage in knowledge. In other words internalization increases the appropriability of the firm's knowledge advantage.

The foreign direct investment case is also illustrated in Figure 3.1, MC is the marginal cost curve for the foreign nation's production (it is the same for host and home country firms producing in that nation). Although MC may differ from that in the home country, as the country specific costs (i.e. production functions) need not be identical between nations, here, for simplicity, it is assumed to be the same. The inter-section of the marginal revenue and marginal cost curves leads to the same equilibrium monopoly quantity of Q^* and price of P^*. The profit from direct investment is given by the area P^*ZF^1F, which is total monopoly profits P^*ZYV less the additional costs FF^1YV to the multinational firm of operating at a distance.

The case of licensing is rather different from the first two. Here the multinational enterprise obtains its profits not directly, but through license fees charged to the foreign firm. But how is the optimal licence fee determined? What is the nature of the costs, if any, of licensing, from the view point of the multinational?

Let us assume that there are several local firms willing to act as licensees for the multinational. Then the multinational firm, holding a knowledge or other special advantage, can act as a monopolist in selling its knowledge. It will sell it at such a price and in such a way as to maximize its licence fees. Since there are several local firms available, they can expect only a normal return on the use of the knowledge, that is, zero economic rent. This means that the local licensee would be willing to give up any monopoly profits it earns in order to obtain the knowledge, up to the point where the profits paid as licence fees would be sufficient to cover the cost of generating the knowledge directly. This alternative cost of knowledge sets a 'limit price' on the licence fee.

For present purposes it is assumed that the monopoly profits in one country alone, the host country, are never sufficient to pay for the cost of generating the knowledge anew. The multinational firm is therefore able to demand a licence fee equal to the full monopoly profit, if any, of the foreign firm. The licensee arrangement that the MNE establishes will then be one which generates the maximum monopoly profit. It will involve only one firm, to ensure a monopoly prevails. Output is set such that marginal revenue equals marginal cost, so the licence fee will be the difference between average revenue (price) and average cost. As before, however, there is a special cost to the multinational associated with this mode of entry, namely D^*.

Figure 3.1 shows the licensing revenues and net profits from licensing. It contains the same host-country demand and normal cost function C^* as before. It differs only in that the net monopolistic profits accruing to the multinational are reduced by special dissipation costs D^* (represented by area LL^1YV) instead of A^*, i.e. the net profits from licensing are area P^*ZL^1L.

The choice between exporting, foreign direct investment and licensing in this model therefore depends entirely on the relative amounts of the export marketing costs M^*, special additional information costs A^* and the dissipation costs D^*. The MNE will find the mode of entry that maximizes profits in the time period.

This one period model can be expressed in algebraic terms, rather than in terms of the diagram used here. This is done by Giddy and

Rugman (1979). The model can then be extended to make the special costs, and other variables, vary with time. The dynamic version on this model is developed in the Giddy and Rugman paper. It leads to the derivation of Figure 3.2 where π represents profits.

Using the solutions of the three reduced form equations from the Giddy-Rugman model it is possible to illustrate the optimal time sequence of entry mode. This is done in Figure 3.2. These profit functions are entirely theoretical, but their relative shapes and time sequences are consistent with the parameters of the three equilibrium equations of the model. Further work is required to test the empirical strength of this model. Several simulations of the model have been undertaken in which values are assigned to the parameters of the reduced form equations such that all the constraints imposed are satisfied. These simulations tend to support the sequence of entry mode illustrated in Figure 3.2.

It is apparent that the dynamics of choice of entry mode in Figure 3.2 are much more complicated than the simple one-period case presented in Figure 3.1. In the static case exporting generates the greatest profits, but if this modality is denied to the firm then FDI is the next best choice, due to the assumption that $A^*<D^*$, which makes licensing the least profitable mode. Yet when special costs (and other variables) vary with time the optimal mode can switch; a typical sequence moving from exporting, to FDI, to licensing. The reasons for this sequence depend on the hypothesis that $M^*<A^*<D^*$, and that they decrease over time in the reverse order (i.e. D^* falls quickest). The importance of these special costs tend to dominate the other variables and become the key determinants of profitability.

In terms of welfare economics it is apparent that in a perfect world (with no information cost) exporting is the first-best option. Yet when the foreign nation imposes a tariff or erects other barriers to entry, then its market can be best serviced by FDI, rather than by host country production by a licensee, provided $A^* < D^*$. The risk aversion of the MNE always sets the licence fee above that charged to its own subsidiary, since with FDI the firm specific advantage is not at risk. Only if the host nation engages in a subsidy to indigenous producers will it be able (eventually) to develop its own knowledge advantage (in its indigenous firms). Otherwise, the host nation is dependent for its technology upon the profit maximizing decisions made by the MNE, which acts in an efficient manner when it overcomes both natural externalities and government induced ones. Only if the MNE endogenizes market imperfections is it being inefficient.

Figure 3.2: The Sequencing of Entry Mode over Time

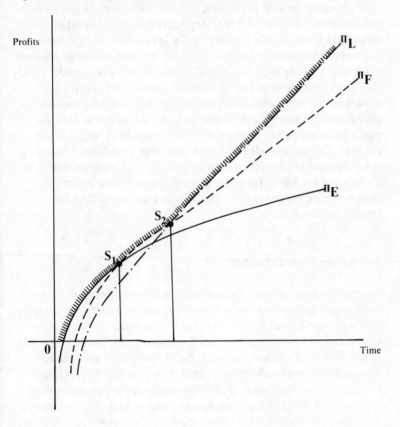

One implication of the model in this section is that the MNE has to take the environmental parameters as given. While exporting is a first-best method in a world of free trade, it is not so attractive when the MNE faces tariff barriers imposed by foreign nations. Such exogenous barriers to trade make it more difficult for the MNE to choose between exporting, FDI and licensing. The MNE would prefer to consider merely the information costs of export marketing versus FDI. Yet its very existence, and the reason for its internal market, may be a response to government imposed market imperfections, such as tariffs. Here the major focus has turned from exogenous costs, such as tariffs, to the relative information costs and risks of the three modalities. Ultimately the exogenous imperfections interact with the cost minimization decisions of the MNE. These interactions are very complex, so this chapter attempted to simplify them by dividing the problem into simpler sub cases.

Alternatives to Internalization

Internalization is just one possible form of organization of allocative mechanisms under conditions of imperfect information, but is likely to be the preferred modality. For simplicity, alternative contractual possibilities have been lumped together here under the heading of licensing. In practice, there are many other forms of contractual arrangements that could be used by the MNE to exploit its firm specific advantage. Future work on the theory of the MNE will explore these alternatives.

The major focus of this work upon internalization and its emphasis upon the FDI modality over the alternatives of exporting and licensing distinguish it from the related work by Dunning (1977, 1979). Dunning believes that an eclectic approach to the theory of the MNE is required; one in which country specific, firm specific ownership advantages, and location theory variables are interrelated. There is considerable overlap between the eclectic approach and internalization theory. One crucial difference arises from the assumption made about the dynamic nature of the firm specific advantage. Is it necessary for the assumption of exogeneity to be retained (as in internalization theory) or can it be assumed to become endogenous at some stage (as in the eclectic approach)?

Dunning argues that the firm specific advantage in knowledge becomes locked into the MNE at some stage. It is transformed into a valuable asset owned by the MNE which acts as a barrier to entry to potential rival firms, i.e. the firm specific advantage has become endogenized. Yet this explanation is consistent with internalization theory, broadly interpreted. The nature of the ownership specific advantage of the MNE as an asset allows the MNE to make its knowledge mobile across national boundaries but permits the use of the knowledge to be safeguarded within the internal market of the MNE. There is no disagreement between the eclectic and internalization theories about the economics of the process of FDI. Where there is room for debate is over the implications to be drawn from the assumption of endogeneity of the ownership advantage. I prefer to isolate the original sourcing of the ownership asset, namely the exogenous market imperfection which encouraged an internal market to develop in the first instance.

The identification of government regulations, tariffs and other controls as unnatural market imperfections is a consistent theme of this book. It has permitted the concept of internalization to be widened from its traditional focus upon natural market imperfections in the pricing of knowledge. A recent paper by Davidson and McFetridge (1980) examines the inefficiencies of the market for transactions in information. Placing emphasis upon work by Williamson (1975) as well as that of Coase they argue that intrafirm exchange is more likely under conditions of information impactedness, bounded rationality and small numbers. They explore conditions under which an intrafirm transfer is the advantageous method of transaction for technology transfer and derive implications which are consistent with internalization theory. Yet they choose to assume that government policies affecting the mode of transfer can be held constant. Thereby they limit the generality of their analysis and fail to examine the unnatural market imperfections which are just as important as the natural ones. Internalization theory needs to be refined to deal with such government imposed exogenous market imperfections.

Dissenting views about the predominance of the FDI modality have been expressed by several writers recently. Buckley and Davis (1979) argue strongly in favour of the licensing option. Casson (1979) identifies plausible conditions under which the transfer of technology follows the licensing route instead of FDI. The former study fails to identify the risk of dissipation of the firm specific advantage as the key characteristic of the licensing modality. The method of FDI avoids this risk, and while it is subject to additional costs (especially in gaining information about the foreign factor as well as goods market) that can be avoided by a licensee, such costs do not put the firm specific advantage of the MNE at risk, as does licensing.

Internalization theory applies to small as well as large MNEs. Both can have firm specific advantages in knowledge, and need to internalize so that all available information on the world environment can be fed into their internal markets. Small MNEs also can benefit from the advantage of international diversification, in contrast to domestic firms, of any size. The possibilities of internalization are unique to the multinational firms (of whatever size) that transcend international market imperfections.

The MNE is a monopolist. It has a firm specific advantage in knowledge (broadly defined as knowledge/technology/management skills etc.) The MNE always seeks to protect this advantage; if it fails to do so it ceases to be a monopolist. Indeed, most MNEs are engaged in ongoing R and D to generate new waves of knowledge. Maintenance of the firm specific advantage in knowledge is best achieved by internalization, since FDI permits the MNE to regulate, monitor, control and otherwise supervise the worldwide disbursement of its knowledge advantage. These incentives to FDI fall only as the product tends to become standardized, or if resale is unlikely to third parties. Even then new waves of innovations by the MNE lead to dynamic forces favouring the FDI modality.

Licensing is a risky modality. The very existence of the MNE is threatened by premature or otherwise inappropriate licensing. Thus the MNE is likely to be risk averse and favour FDI over licensing. Freely transferable property rights in an advantage are required for licensing to work yet, in general, these do not exist. If a property right is transferable it is no longer likely to reflect any real firm specific advantage. Monopolists cannot transfer their attributes without the grave risk of dissipation of the advantage. Property rights were assigned to the MNE in the first place to solve Magee's appropriability problem. They need to remain firm specific and are not readily marketable. There is always likely to be some difficulty in negotiating the correct licence fee. Either or both parties may have incorrect forecasts about the future probable value of the knowledge advantage. The risk is greater for the MNE.

There is no 'market' for proprietary information in the generally accepted use of the term. There are no homogenous products being priced; indeed there is no price per unit of knowledge. The 'market' does not exist as a common good. Instead all we observe are the results of specific deals. The deals are likely to be secretive as they are based on intelligence not generally available outside the firms involved. It is very hard to price intangible information on a regular market. While contractual arrangements could be negotiated in theory, in practice the internal market of the MNE is likely to be a superior method of servicing foreign markets. FDI avoids the problem of incorrect pricing and is thus risk free. Patents are not readily enforceable internationally, so the MNE is a better mode.

The costs of policing a licence can be high. This cost of enforcement has to be added to insurance costs (which one or both parties have to pay). Under internalization both types of costs are avoided. The full risk of dissipation of the firm specific advantage in knowledge cannot be avoided by even a carefully designed contract. By its very nature a firm specific advantage is not readily separable from the firm. It is not diffusable unless embodied in a process or product made by the MNE. But then the process or product generally makes use of the other attributes of the internal market of the MNE, so how are these characteristics to be separated and priced accordingly? All in all the correct pricing of information is a very difficult job; one which many contractual arrangements fail to do properly.

It is essential to recognize that each MNE is a monopolist in its use of knowledge (or some other firm specific advantage). Otherwise the MNE does not need either an internal market *or* a contractual arrangement. When there is no monopoly in knowledge then a regular market suffices. Similarly, MNEs compete for final markets but each MNE uses its internal market in knowledge to put some shape on its demand curve by the process of product differentiation. There is no need for any special theory of the MNE when competitive markets occur. Indeed, then international trade theory is alone sufficient to determine international production. But information is an intermediate product not explained very well by trade theory; it is better explained by the theory of the firm. Information can be viewed as an intermediate product that has both a stock and flow component nurtured by both past and ongoing R and D.

John Dunning has supported the emphasis placed by Peter Buckley on licensing and further suggests that intermediate forms of international involvement need to be incorporated into the theory of the MNE. There are contractual arrangements which are neither equity investment (FDI) nor off-the-shelf arm's-length transactions (licensing); examples arise in the mining and hotel industries.

Yet the question to be asked is to what extent the mining and hotel industries offer standardized products (easy to license) but with no 'advantage', or products/services with a genuine knowledge advantage. Only the latter are of concern here. What, then, is the unique firm specific advantage of an MNE in the hotel industry? It must be associated with an ability to product differentiate (advertising and/or special services) in an otherwise fairly standardized industry. Once a monopoly advantage is achieved then franchises in the hotel chain can be sold, provided suitable contractual arrangements can be worked out. There remains a risk of dissipation of the firm specific advantage if one of the licensees provides inferior service, so the hotel chain still needs to monitor and regulate the use of its advantage. Whether it can do this better by a contractual arrangement or by an internal market is the issue.

In general, internalization theory predicts that the more vulnerable the unique firm specific advantage of the hotel chain to imitation, then the greater the incentive for an internal market. As the risk of dissipation falls the opportunity for appropriate and mutually beneficial contractual arrangements increases at the expense of the internal market. There is no point in doing licensing if substantial post-contractual control is required; instead full control can be exercised by the internal market. The need for intermediate involvement and post-contractual control will be reduced as the firm specific advantage becomes more standardized.

In the mining industry, as Hymer (1976) first recognized, the firm specific advantage of the MNE arises from control of the raw material source. The resource-based MNEs are somewhat different from manufacturing MNEs, since the latter need to make a technological knowledge advantage by R and D expenditures. The mining MNEs use an internal market to integrate backwards to the raw material and, often, forwards, to process and market the resource product. While contractual arrangements are possible in the mining industry they will not be as feasible as internalization since it is difficult to segment the stages by which the firm specific advantage is secured. For example, is a geologist or a salesman of greater value to a mineral resource MNE? Both exploration and marketing are essential elements and they may well be inseparable.

Intermediate involvement in non-equity investment is neither necessary nor viable in the mining industry. Why have intermediate involvement (where is the 'intermediate' cut off point anyway?) when the internal market guarantees full and proper control? There is a risk of loss of control in any contractual arrangement, no matter how carefully negotiated. As circumstances change it is dangerous to be locked into a prior agreement. The internal market is a superior alternative to non-equity involvement because it is a flexible market with which the MNE can adjust to external changes. Such evolution is extremely difficult to foresee and write into a successful contractual

agreement. On the other hand an internal market can be either formal
or informal; it depends on the preferences of the management team of
the MNE. Flexibility and control are the attributes of an internal
market; they permit the firm specific advantage to be monitored as
desired by the MNE.

In conclusion, we can anticipate that the next development of the
theory of the multinational enterprise, with its emphasis upon the
organization of an internal market, will be to incorporate recent developments in non-equity forms of international involvement into the theory
of the MNE. Such contractual arrangements are of increasing importance
in international production and marketing. They include, licensing, joint
ventures and forms of intermediate involvement where some degree of
post contractual control is retained.

It has been demonstrated here that the negotiation of a contractual
agreement for a non-standardized product is a very difficult task. There
is a danger that the firm specific advantage (in knowledge, technology,
organization, managerial or marketing skills) may be dissipated by the
use of non-equity forms of international involvement. It is apparent
that incorrect prices for proprietary information are likely to be
negotiated in contractual agreements which lack the discipline of
market constraints.

It has been found that the internal market of the MNE is a superior
device to non-equity forms of international involvement, as the costs
of internalization are less than the costs of contracting. The costs of
internalization depend on first, the organization of an effective com-
munications network within the MNE and, secondly, the additional
costs of social distance and political risk associated with entry to an
unfamiliar foreign environment. These costs are high enough to have
eliminated any excess profits from the earnings of the 50 largest US
and 50 largest non-US MNEs. Over the 1970-9 period only six US
MNEs had a return on equity of 18 per cent or more (i.e. 50 per cent
above the all-industry mean return of 12 per cent) but these were offset
by a group of MNEs earning 50 per cent below the mean. (For further
details see Tables 7.1 and 7.2.)

The costs of non-equity forms of involvement include the risk of
dissipation of the firm specific advantage by the premature or inappropriately priced sale of knowledge and the danger of loss of control
over the use of the firm's knowledge advantage by a poorly conceived
contractual arrangement. The visible costs of contracting include the
costs of policing the licence or other non-equity form of involvement
plus the costs of insurance which have to be paid for by either or

both parties to the contractual agreement.

It is concluded that non-equity forms of international involvement are increasing due to: (a) the growth of standardized products (b) the increasing segmentation of world goods and factor markets which makes resale to third parties a more difficult task and (c) the increased amount of government regulation of foreign direct investment and the MNE, which acts to increase the incentive for contractual arrangements with local participation. There are probably welfare losses involved in the forced substitution of contracts for internal markets, in the same way that the denial of exporting imposed costs of foregone efficiency on returns in the past.

4 IMPLICATIONS OF THE THEORY OF INTERNALIZATION FOR CORPORATE INTERNATIONAL FINANCE

Internalization of Financial Market Imperfections

Several of the concepts from corporate international finance may need to be rethought once the theory of internalization is accepted as a general theory of foreign direct investment (FDI). It can be seen that the modifications to corporate international finance theory developed in this chapter fall into a common pattern and that internalization serves to unify and integrate many of the existing areas of the field. This common pattern emerges once attention is directed towards the imperfect nature of international financial markets.

The theory of international production can be extended in an important direction by recognizing that imperfect financial markets exist in addition to imperfect goods and factor markets. Although it has been traditional to assume that international financial markets are well integrated it should be recognized that they are not perfectly integrated. This is due primarily to regulations on capital movements between nations. In fact, most countries impose capital controls and taxes on international monetary transactions for balance of payments reasons.

Given that there is not a perfect international capital market, an important implication arises for the theory of internalization. It is now well known that there are gains to be made from holding an efficient portfolio of international assets. It follows that individuals with risk aversion in their utility functions will seek to reduce the systematic risk of any one nation's market portfolio by searching for appropriate international assets, and that they will desire to purchase shares in foreign corporations as well as to hold other foreign assets.

Since there are barriers to international diversification by financial investment these individuals will be frustrated as they seek to construct an efficient international portfolio of shares and assets. Instead, they can either purchase shares in world mutual funds, or in multinational enterprises (MNEs). The world mutual funds may still be faced by national financial market barriers which only an MNE can overcome. It is able to produce in various nations, and use its internal accounts to transmit to the parent firm the advantages of stable international production. In this manner the MNE is a vehicle for international diversification. The

75

MNE is engaged in internalization in the financial market in much the same way as it internalizes the goods and factor markets for information.

The theme of this section is that international production occurs in response to imperfect markets in information and knowledge by internalization, i.e. the MNE creates a market within its own organizational structure. This section will develop theoretical applications of internalization in three areas of imperfect international markets:

(a)   in control of the information,
(b)   in international locations of the information,
(c)   in international transfer (trade) of the information.

These three areas can be integrated into a general theory of international production once it is realized that the common element to each of them is the lack of an efficient market. This is the crucial factor motivating the analysis of internalization as it applies to international finance.

It is found that internal marketing of information by an MNE can be an efficient substitute for an external market. There are interesting distributional effects, but no general finding that the MNE can appropriate surplus profits when it acts as an agent for information transfer.

Many others have written about the imperfections in international financial markets (that is, the degree of segmentation or integration of national capital markets)—for recent surveys see Aliber (1978b) and Lessard (1979). Here it is simply assumed that the international capital market is not perfectly integrated (in contrast to the domestic capital market of the United States, or any other major industrialized nation, which is assumed to be perfect). The degree of capital market imperfection is relatively unimportant in this study, since the general principle of internalization of markets comes into force once any segmentation of the international capital market (or, indeed, any other relevant externality) is recognized.

In this chapter it would be a feasible method of presentation to consider the application of the theory of internalization to each of the major areas of corporate international finance. For example, given that the unique risk facing the MNE, compared to a domestic corporation, is foreign exchange risk then the first apparent application would be to hedging, speculation and arbitrage. Yet we know that the foreign exchange market functions as if it were an efficient market, in the sense that new information affecting currency values is reflected in relative exchange rates very quickly—see Dufey and Giddy (1978).

Therefore, internalization (which breeds upon market imperfections rather than efficient markets) does not explain the activities of an MNE in the foreign exchange market. Indeed, internalization is more likely to be associated with the argument that the MNE should largely ignore its accounting exposure to exchange rate variations and instead should focus only upon its economic exposure.

Rather than continue to list the areas in which internalization may provide new insights into the general issues of corporate international finance this chapter proceeds to investigate some of the more interesting ones, leaving the others for future development. The major areas explored are: international diversification, transfer pricing and the financial structure of the MNE, including its cost of capital and finance function.

Application to international banking and capital sourcing for the MNE is also feasible, but such work is reserved for a later chapter. However, in this connection the efforts by Dufey and Giddy (1978) to explain the development of the Eurocurrency market as a response to regulation and control of the domestic US banking system is of particular relevance. Although they do not consider the theory of internalization *per se*, their argument that regulation of US domestic financial inter- mediaries leads to the growth of the Eurocurrency market, where the Eurobanks can operate on a narrower spread due to the lack of regulation (among other factors), is an example of an efficient institutional response to imperfect markets. The very existence of the Eurocurrency market confirms the ability of multinational banks to overcome imperfections (that is, regulations and controls) in domestic financial markets, in an efficient manner. This process of generating firm specific (or bank specific) organizational ability, knowledge and information advantages – to overcome imperfect markets – is the essence of internalization.

The Links Between the Foreign Exchange and Stock Markets

There have been several studies of the efficiency of the foreign exchange market in recent years. Notable contributions include those by: Dufey and Giddy (1978), Giddy (1977b), Levich (1979), Cornell (1977) and Aliber (1978a). Some of these authors have attempted weak form and semi-strong form tests of the efficient markets hypothesis. They have found that the foreign exchange market is efficient in the sense that it absorbs rapidly any new information generated by exogenous shocks. Important implications of this finding about the efficiency of foreign exchange markets (ignoring the many qualifications) are that forecasting is uncalled for, that there remain no profitable opportunities for exchange speculation and that the forward exchange rate is an unbiased predictor of the expected future spot exchange rate.

At the same time there have been studies undertaken of the share prices of multinational enterprises (MNEs), mainly in the context of international diversification. Recent works include those by Hughes *et al.* (1975), Agmon and Lessard (1977), Rugman (1977b, 1979), Senchack and Beedles (1978) and Elliott (1978). In general, this literature has ignored the effect of foreign exchange risk, a simplification which is readily achieved by converting rates of return on foreign stock indices, and individual corporation returns, into US dollars or some other convenient numeraire when applying the market model or international versions of the capital asset pricing model. The studies have tended to find significant differences in the betas of MNEs compared with uninational firms. Some of the studies have found that the MNEs are vehicles for international diversification. There is some evidence of the superior performance of MNEs in the stock market, although the evidence is mixed.

Ayarslan (1980) makes use of these two strands of literature, although he does not contribute to either directly. Instead, a new approach is tried; one which examines the impact of currency realignments (and their implications for foreign exchange risk) upon the way the domestic US stock market values the share of MNE. Therefore foreign exchange risk is not examined in the foreign exchange market itself, but in the stock market performance of MNEs versus uninational firms. The efficiency of the foreign exchange market is assumed and only the impact of foreign exchange risk (due to exchange rate changes) on MNEs is examined. There has been little work along these lines, except for one or two studies. Ayarslan finds the 1973 US devaluation was not fully anticipated in the stock market.

In his doctoral dissertation Giddy (1974) explained the impact of exchange rate changes on stock prices, over the 1967-73 period, for seven stock markets, which include both MNEs and uninational firms. In his aggregative study Giddy postulated an inverse relationship between exchange rate changes and the national stock index, such that a devaluation is likely to be affected by appreciation in the aggregate stock prices of that nation. Giddy looked mainly at stock indices and did not distinguish between MNEs and uninational firms. He relied upon a residual analysis of stock indices.

Of related interest, is the literature on the foreign exchange exposure of MNEs and the specific impact of accounting versus economic exposure. Recent studies by Dukes (1980) and by Folks and Evans (1980) have examined the impact of FASB Statement Number 8 on the share prices of MNEs. These are reported and discussed in the recent book by Levich and Wihlborg (1980).

The next part of this chapter explains the implications of imperfections in international financial markets, where the information content of foreign exchange rate changes is reflected in stock prices, but where individual investors are prevented from direct purchase of shares and therefore cannot enjoy the benefits of international diversification.

International Diversification and Internalization

Due to the lack of perfect integration of international capital markets there are opportunities for an investor to benefit from international diversification. The potential gains from international diversification were first recognized by Grubel (1968) and have been confirmed in several subsequent studies, as reported in Rugman (1977a, b, 1979). These, and other studies identify a lack of perfect correlation among the returns of stock indices of various nations. This finding implies that national investor risk can be reduced by holding an efficient portfolio of both domestic and foreign assets.

Although these gains exist in theory it is not clear that an investor can realize them in practice. This is particularly true when the investor is not just buying into a stock index but is engaged in the purchase of shares of foreign corporations (along with domestic ones) to include in an efficient world portfolio. The construction of such a portfolio of corporate assets is beset with difficulties.

First, the investor faces information and search costs in the acquisition of knowledge about foreign corporations. Although some relevant knowledge can be purchased from specialized agencies, i.e. if the knowledge services can be rented by the investor, it is difficult to tailor such information to the specific requirements of the investor's unique tastes. Further, transactions and brokerage costs are likely to be greater for international assets compared to domestic ones.

Secondly, the investor is exposed to foreign exchange risk should it be necessary to bring home the realized gains of foreign investments. It is both difficult to predict the future course of the exchange rates of nations in which the investor has purchased corporate shares, and also to evaluate the impact of such risks on the portfolio. It might be argued that each nation's stock market is efficient in the sense that the information content of foreign exchange changes are incorporated in the valuation of shares.

While it is probably correct that the stock markets of most advanced nations are, indeed, efficient in terms of the semi-strong form of the efficient markets hypothesis, it is not so clear that the stock markets of some of the developing nations of the southern hemisphere can satisfy this condition. Thus, the individual investor faces foreign exchange risk if it becomes necessary to sell out parts of his world portfolio, or realize dividend yields on foreign shareholdings. No insurance can be bought against this risk so it must be offset against the expected return on international asset holdings. This is a practical argument against international diversification, which does not invalidate the point that the investor should buy the market factors (of various nations) and hold. This theoretical prescription is clearly not of relevance in this discussion of the problems of achieving individual international diversification.

Thirdly, the investor faces existing and unexpected changes in tax laws and possible foreign exchange controls which may be imposed by both foreign and home governments. For example, the US Interest Equalization Tax made it virtually impossible for a private US investor to benefit from his own international diversification until it was abolished in 1973. There are undoubtedly other examples of government regulations and special taxes which affect international capital flows. What is common to them all is that they are examples of financial market imperfections.

The international capital market is not perfect, unlike the internal capital markets of specific nations. It is due to these very imperfections that some of the opportunities for international diversification arise. The remaining opportunities exist due to the lack of perfect positive correlation of real economic activities, such as trade cycles, labour strikes, mineral discoveries, poor harvests and so on. These real economic activities are reflected eventually in the national financial markets and they contribute to the generation of a unique systematic risk for each and every nation. The special attraction of international diversification is that it permits an investor to escape in part the systematic risk of the domestic nation. Given the difficulties facing an investor in constructing an efficient world portfolio of stocks, what can be done?

One alternative is to purchase shares in a world mutual fund. The number of these institutional facilities is increasing, with many of them using the services of international banks to gather information on foreign economies and corporations. The world mutual funds still face the tax, governmental regulation and foreign exchange risk barriers that confront the individual, but they may be a little better placed to overcome them. Some investors may still find it uneconomical to attempt to achieve the benefits of international diversification through the purchase of shares in world mutual funds, perhaps because of home country banking and investment regulations, or due to the service charges of the fund. Such individuals have a third option, namely to purchase shares in truly multinational corporations traded on their domestic stock exchanges.

The role of the MNE as a vehicle for international diversification in a world of barriers to individual international investment is analyzed in Rugman (1979), so that work is not fully repeated here. Yet it is of interest to note that the ability of the MNE to offer the benefits of stable earnings to its investors is due to its foreign production and sales which generate a more stable pattern of sales over time than can be enjoyed by purely domestic corporations, whatever industry they are in. To an extent the MNE links up the economic benefits of stable sales and earnings with the financial effects of a superior stock market performance when compared to domestic firms. By superior performance is meant less risk (as measured either by variance or beta) for the same level of expected return – see Rugman (1979). The investor is interested only in the financial stock market opportunities for international diversification but these exist only due to the physical international operations of the MNE. In this sense the MNE transcends the boundaries of its domestic stock market and brings home to individual domestic investors the fruits of international stability.

It should also be remembered that the motivation of the MNE in making each physical overseas investment comes from market imperfections, such as tariff and taxes which destroy exports, or the public good nature of its knowledge advantage which denies licensing as a viable option. The MNE is engaged in the process of internalization. It is a creature of imperfect markets. In turn, the MNE offers to individuals the benefits of international diversification. Thus, the MNE combines in itself both internalization and international diversification advantages. In doing so it links them up and provides an attractive investment package to individuals starved of assets for their desired world portfolios.

In his now classic survey of the theory of foreign direct investment (FDI) Professor John Dunning (1973) paid scant attention to the topic of international portfolio diversification. In the subsequent time period research on this important area of FDI has bounded ahead. It has been shown, on both theoretical and empirical grounds, that the multinational enterprise (MNE) is a surrogate for individual international diversification in a world of segmented capital markets. The advantages of risk reduction are an interesting new reason in attempting to explain the motivation of international production. This section offered a summary and synthesis of recent work on international portfolio diversification and suggested how it may be integrated into the new theory of internalization.

Buckley and Casson (1976) on the subject of portfolio theory and diversification through foreign direct investment, 'argue that the theory which applies to an individual investor cannot be applied to a corporate direct investor such as an MNE' (p. 82). In defence of this opinion they advanced two arguments: first, that individual shareholders of an MNE can undertake portfolio diversification themselves and only require corporate diversification if there are barriers to individual diversification. The second objection is that the holding of a controlling interest by an MNE will involve an excessive part of its total portfolio being confined to a single large, indivisible asset.

These statements are questionable on both grounds. Due to barriers to international investment such as taxes and foreign exchange controls individuals of many nations (including the UK when Buckley and Casson were writing) are usually denied the opportunity of portfolio diversification. It is frequently legally or prohibitively expensive for individuals to purchase shares of foreign corporations. Given that these barriers usually exist, the option of doing it privately is just not available. The second argument is an error of perception, since while a large interest by the MNE is required for control, this constraint does not apply to an individual investor. Instead shares can be bought in the MNE, and an optimal portfolio (for the individual) constructed.

To summarize, the theory of internalization can also be applied to the area of international diversification. The recent literature on international diversification has demonstrated a superior stock market performance for MNEs compared to uninational firms, after allowing for size and industry differences. This superior performance is due partly to the advantage possessed by the MNE in its exploitation of information through an internal market. The role of the MNE as a surrogate vehicle for individual international diversification in a world of capital market imperfections is intimately related to its ability to create an internal market which bypasses such imperfections. Here again the MNE is responding in an efficient manner to an exogenous market imperfection.

Transfer Pricing and Internalization

It has been established on theoretical grounds that the MNE has the ability to use transfer prices and that these may increase the overall profit rate of the firm. One of the best demonstrations of this, using a heuristic programming technique, is by Nieckels (1976). He extends the original work of Hirschleifer (1956), Gould (1964) and others, done in a domestic context, to an international dimension and proves that the performance of an MNE is improved by the use of transfer prices.

Similar conclusions, using rigorous linear programming or other analytical models, have been reached by Horst (1971, 1977), Copithorne (1971), Booth and Jensen (1977), Eden (1978) and Lessard (1979). The last mentioned writer has also recognized that transfer pricing by the MNE takes place in a world of imperfect markets. Here this insight is extended further and an even stronger interpretation is made; namely, that transfer prices are an efficient response by the MNE to exogenous market imperfections.

The MNE has to operate in a world characterized by international tax rate differentials, foreign exchange controls, currency manipulation, multiple exchange rates, governmental regulations and barriers to investment. Such market imperfections erect high transactions costs for the international firm if it uses regular markets. To avoid these externalities and other excessive costs it creates an internal market. The MNE then uses administrative fiat to allocate resources, intermediate products and other factors between its parent division and the foreign subsidiaries. In this process of internalization it is natural that internal (transfer) prices be used. Such prices are set by administrative decision and have to be respected as the prices necessary to make the MNE function efficiently.

Turning attention to the pricing of an intermediate good such as knowledge or information, as embodied in the products of an MNE, let a transfer price be defined as a non-market price set internally by an MNE. If a proper market existed for information there could be an arm's length price, but since there is no market the MNE determined the price of information by use of its internal pricing.

The need for an internal market always remains in the valuation of information, and transfer prices for this intermediate product are justified. In this context transfer prices probably follow a random walk, that is, they respond in a weakly efficient manner to random shocks in the generation of new knowledge and information. In this view the internal prices used by the organization of the MNE are set by administrative fiat and incorporate all relevant information about exogenous economic and financial conditions.

Many critics of the MNE point out that transfer prices may well not equal 'arm's length' or market prices. There are at least two errors in such criticism.

First, the so-called arm's length prices do not exist. When there is no (external) market there is no market price. Conversely, when there is an internal market created by the MNE within its own organization then the resulting transfer prices are the correct ones. Without them the internal market might not exist, so the MNE is entitled to charge whatever prices it wishes for intermediate products provided it produces final goods which can be sold openly. The ultimate control over transfer pricing comes in the market for the final product of the MNE, since an inefficient performance, due to incorrect transfer pricing, will lead eventually to the demise of the MNE.

Secondly, the transfer prices are created by the MNE in response to market imperfections. If governments regard transfer pricing as a potential abuse of the power of MNEs then there is a ready solution at hand. This is to harmonize international tax rates, eliminate exchange controls and other barriers to capital flows imposed by governments. Such a first-best solution will remove the incentive for transfer pricing of MNEs.

The empirical work of Vaitsos (1974), Lall (1973) and others has found evidence of transfer pricing, mainly in the pharmaceuticals industry in Colombia. They also find that the profits of subsidiaries in Latin America are 'squeezed' by the parent MNEs. In another study Rugman (1980f) finds no evidence of transfer pricing as reflected in the earnings performance between the parents and subsidiaries of US MNEs active in the Canadian mineral resource industry. While some subsidiaries have low profits, and others higher profits, there is no significant difference after adjusting for risk of earnings.

This ambiguity in the empirical work is in sharp contrast to the theoretical work referenced earlier which finds that MNEs can use transfer pricing. It appears that, in practice, transfer pricing is hard to find so its abuse by the MNEs must be left in question. Further, the MNE must find it difficult to set a price for intangibles such as knowledge generation, technological advantage and managerial skills, so there are probably no 'correct' transfer prices anyhow. Thus the theory of internalization reveals that the internal pricing of knowledge advantages by the MNE is merely a response to the lack of a market. It is not a suspicious action but a rational one by an efficient business organization, the MNE.

The use of transfer pricing for tangible goods which can be priced in a recognized external market would be defensible, in any case, if the MNE responded to an exogenous market imperfection, such as differentials in national tax rates. The tax policies of governments are not uniform so the MNE is presented with an opportunity to minimize its tax bill by using transfer prices in its intra-company accounting. If tax rates are equalized internationally then there is no incentive for transfer pricing by the MNE (assuming that no other capital market imperfections exist).

Transfer prices are not arbitrary numbers but are the correct internal administrative prices required to make internalization function. It is meaningless to examine transfer prices on their own, or to attempt to compare them to non-existent arm's length prices. Instead the MNE should be allowed to use whatever transfer prices it cares to. Only its performance in producing final goods is of interest to consumer and governments. Thus the overall profits of MNEs should be analyzed rather than partial aspects of the firm such as transfer pricing.

Mathewson and Quirin (1979) undertake a rigorous theoretical and empirical treatment of transfer price manipulation by multinational corporations (MNEs) operating in Canada. The authors first develop a model with Cobb-Douglas production functions for several intermediate processes used in a final product sold in two countries. They calculate costs of labour and capital for these processes and find that in 1979 labour costs are a little lower in Canada than in the USA, but that the cost of capital is significantly higher, reflecting a greater perceived risk of the Canadian economy. Next they introduce tariffs and taxes and it is found that 'transfer pricing erodes the effect of the tariff', and that the MNE can use internal prices to minimize the distortions of international tax rate differentials. Extending the model to three countries does not change these findings.

The authors' empirical work is based upon the more general constant elasticity of substitution (CES) production functions. Due to lack of company data on transfer pricing practices of MNEs, the authors are forced to assume parameter values for their empirical analysis. The data problem is compounded by the difficulty of setting a price for intangibles and managerial services which are provided within the internal market of the MNE, but do not exist on a regular (competitive) market. The authors state that as many as 25,000 cases have been examined using their CES-based computer programme. The more interesting results are reported in a detailed appendix. On the basis of this exhaustive theoretical and empirical research work the authors conclude 'that multinationals have a relatively restricted scope for transfer price manipulation'.

Internalization and the Financial Structure of the MNE

One of the first applications of internalization is to the cost of capital of the MNE. Internalization explains why the appropriate cost of capital for the MNE is that of the MNE itself and not that of the individual subsidiaries. This point has been demonstrated by Shapiro (1978) and Giddy (1977a). My interpretation of their work is that the MNE is creating an internal market for information on project evaluation, after adjusting for risk considerations. The MNE is able to overcome segmented international capital markets and within its own organizational structure it can operate an efficient market. It is as if the MNE itself becomes a proxy for an integrated capital market. If the MNE did not have an efficient internal market then each segment of it (each subsidiary) would have to generate an independent cost of capital.

This insight implies that the cost of capital for foreign subsidiaries should not be determined independently, nor should specific project evaluations have their own required rates of return set without consideration being given to the effects of the project on the overall MNE. There is a common (capital) market within the MNE and all projects and subsidiaries are integrated parts of the firm.

Internalization can also explain why joint ventures are often inferior to production by wholly-owned subsidiaries. The MNE is able to appropriate a fair return on its investment in research only if it can subsequently use its own organization to use the information advantage. The information monopoly secured by the internal market of an MNE is threatened once a local partner is acquired, since there may be disclosure of the unique research advantage embodied within the MNE. These last points are developed at more length in the paper by Giddy and Rugman (1979).

In a similar fashion the concept of internalization can help to explain why a centralized finance function is required by the MNE, a point made in Robbins and Stobaugh (1973). In order to control information about foreign exchange risk and to exploit opportunities for arbitrage and speculation, the management of international finance must be centralized. Once a centralized finance function is being used, it is then necessary to evaluate the performance of the MNE as a whole and not that of subsidiaries in isolation. Also, the accounting implications of exogenous regulations, such as FASB Standard Number 8, should be of secondary importance and economic exposure alone be of concern to an MNE operating an internal market.

The MNE can purchase some information on foreign exchange movements and currency risks but it must judge the impact of international factors for itself. The exposure of the MNE to foreign exchange risk and political risk can be found by an assessment of the profitability of the overall MNE. The MNE is an integrated unit straddling national boundaries which benefits from an internal market. The costs of exchange risk, if any, are often misunderstood. It is often argued that the MNE is subject to either accounting exposure or economic exposure and that foreign exchange risk may affect the share valuation of MNEs. In this case economic exposure is of more relevance than accounting exposure and it is an empirical question to test the possible differential share price performance of multinational versus uninational firms.

The MNE is a creature of the world economy. It operates in different nations, many of which have their own currencies. Foreign exchange rates are set, or influenced, by the central banks of the home and host nations, not by the MNEs, who are interested in the use of foreign exchange for transactions purposes rather than speculative ones. The exposure of MNEs to foreign exchange risk is not a problem in itself, and should not be treated as one. Instead the MNE should determine its long run profit maximization strategy by producing and selling in optimal locations, that is, its economic decisions should include exchange risk as only one element in the location decision.

The theory of internalization has not yet been fully incorporated into academic research on the efficiency of foreign exchange markets and the impact of foreign exchange risk (if any) on the MNE. As stated above it is necessary to examine the effect of exchange risk on the stock prices of MNEs. This can be done by applying the capital asset pricing model to the MNE, using a US market based index as the market factor. The US index is appropriate since it is necessary to test the response of the US stock market, by its own shares valuations, to the perceived exchange risk affecting MNEs. (In contrast when international diversification is the subject of interest it is more useful to apply a proxy world market factor rather than a US index alone, since the latter is only part of the international capital market, although highly correlated with it.)

Once appropriate tests of the effects of exchange risk on the share prices of US based MNEs have been made it will be possible to evaluate the importance of internalization in this area. It is necessary to examine the information content of foreign exchange rate changes as they affect stock market prices. Some tests of this semi-strong form of the efficient markets hypothesis have been made by Giddy (1974). At this moment the state of the art is one where the conceptual case for internalization can be made, but this theoretical proposition still lacks empirical confirmation (or rejection).

Conclusions

In summary, the theme of this chapter is that internalization applies to corporate international finance not only as an explanation of the motives for FDI, but also as a description of the internal operations and management structure of the MNE. The theory of internalization thereby helps to throw new light on several specific areas of corporate international finance, as discussed above.

5 MULTINATIONAL BANKING AND THE THEORY OF INTERNALIZATION

The Theory of Multinational Banking

This chapter applies the theory of internalization to explain the activities of international banks. It has already been established that multinational banks have stable earnings, see Rugman (1979) Chapter 12 and Khoury (1980). What are the reasons for such a good performance? Are they to be found in the international environment, external to the multinational bank, or are they internal? Here it is argued that the latter explanation of earnings stability is of great importance. Indeed, the theory of internalization, used successfully in analysis of the multinational enterprise elsewhere in this book can also be applied to the activities of multinational banks. It is shown here that multinational banks act as vehicles for the internalization of imperfections in international financial markets and that they provide specialized information services which are not otherwise available to multinational enterprises.

Both multinational banks and multinational enterprises are organizations that use administrative fiat to clear internal markets. As explained earlier, the multinational enterprise is forced to create an internal market for the pricing of intermediate products such as knowledge, research and firm specific managerial skills. These inputs into its final product are not priced in a regular market since they represent externalities to the standard neoclassical market system. When there are Coasian-type transactions costs facing a multinational firm in some of its activities, it will decide to undertake them internally when this is cheaper than using a regular market, for example when knowledge cannot be purchased on a market, as it is a public good, or when the multinational firm needs to establish property rights over innovations to appropriate a fair return for related prior expenditures on research and development.

Like domestic banks the multinational banks are active in the compilation, processing and use of information. The control and application of information lies at the heart of banking, since financial intermediation is a process in which the bank centralizes information used by borrowers and lenders. The indirect securities offered by a bank incorporate the informational advantages of financial intermediation. Viewed in this light, the diversification opportunities presented by a bank are attributes of the superior information skills embodied in that institution compared to individuals or corporations which do not specialize in financial knowledge.

Unlike domestic banks, multinational banks benefit from the additional advantage of international diversification. The domestic banks specialize in the assembly of financial information used for intermediation in one economy. The earnings of these domestic banks are subject to the systematic risk of that nation's domestic economy and stock markets, to the extent that the nation is isolated from international trade and capital movements. In the case of self sufficient nations and segmented capital markets, a domestic bank is entirely dependent upon its local market and its performance will reflect that of the domestic economy. The profits and share valuations for the domestic bank are derived from the local markets serviced. Domestic banks are also subject to the specific regulations of their domestic banking system and they are unable to escape the shackles of such regulation.

On the other hand multinational banks operate on an international basis and are free of system specific regulations since there exists no world central bank or world government with the authority to control multinational banks. They escape the systematic risk of any one national market, as can the multinational enterprise. Therefore the earnings of multinational banks should be (and are) more stable than domestic banks, due to the unique advantage of international diversification enjoyed by the multinational banks over national banks. These benefits are reinforced by the principle of internalization since the multinational banks can overcome the usual imperfections in the market for information, in this case financial information. As they do so, multinational banks generate a firm specific internal advantage in the use of such information. In the same way that the multinational enterprise creates an internal market to overcome imperfect world goods and factor markets so does the multinational bank use internalization to overcome imperfections in international financial markets. These imperfections occur whenever national capital markets are not perfectly integrated. In practice, this condition is generally satisfied, so there is always an opening for internalization available to the multinational bank. The process of internalization is complementary to that of international diversification. The multinational bank benefits from both, the domestic bank from neither.

The capital market within any single country is assumed to be perfect for the purpose of this analysis. Indeed a national currency area can be defined as one within which capital is perfectly mobile. In this case there is a common price for capital in different regions, that is, interest rates are the same between regions of a nation, since the financial system has arbitraged the domestic money market. In addition there is a single, uniform, exchange rate between any nation's currency unit and those of foreign countries. The central bank attempts to regulate domestic monetary policy and monitors the common (to all regions within a nation) foreign exchange rate. Under these conditions a domestic bank operates in a perfect capital market, subject to the systematic risk of that nation. However, this national currency area is separated from other ones, so a multinational bank situated in this nation, compared to a domestic bank, can gain from international operations, since only the multinational bank has the opportunity of going abroad (in its service activities and financial activities) to diversify.

Within any nation there are no remaining opportunities for a domestic bank to benefit from either international diversification or internalization. The former (diversification) is denied by definition of a national currency area and its supportive, indeed protective, domestic banking system. The latter (internalization) is not available to the domestic bank to the same extent as it is to a multinational bank since the size of any national market must always be smaller than that of the world market. Any ownership specific advantages of a bank are better exploited in the world market than in the domestic market alone. In addition, internalization is more useful on an international scale, since there are many more potential financial market imperfections to be overcome between countries, given the propensity for governments to erect barriers to free capital movements as they attempt to regulate the balance of payments and achieve other national economic objectives.

It is much cheaper for the multinational bank to acquire financial information about world capital markets than it is for the multinational enterprise to overcome the additional costs of foreign goods and factor markets. To this extent alone operations by multinational banks should be either more profitable, or less risky, than those of multinational enterprises. In short, multinational banks do better than domestic banks (since these miss out on the net benefits of international banking) and multinational enterprises (since they have greater additional costs of subsidiary production than do the banks).

Internalization and its effects on multinational banks is related to scale economies, degree of market power as measured by industry concentration ratio, regulatory protection, and so on. Both domestic and multinational banks will compete in the home economy and the effect of any of these considerations upon their performance cannot be uniquely distinguished. The regulations affecting the domestic and international financial systems are best assumed to be exogenous, as is the structure of the economy itself. The more efficient type of bank (either domestic or multinational) will grow fastest and one or the other group may even increase its share of the home market, but probably not in any dramatic fashion. The real difference between domestic and multinational banks is that the latter have more scope for growth and profitability through international operations.

A Summary of Multinational Banking Theory

To summarize the key point, multinational banks enjoy the same benefits available to the multinational enterprises, namely the twin opportunities of internalization and international diversification. Yet, as the multinational bank specializes in the processing of financial information alone, the potential advantages of international banking are probably greater than those of international production and sales by the multinational firm. This is due to the additional costs of operating in foreign factor and goods markets, costs which are incurred by the multinational enterprise by virtue of its role as a producer, but costs which are avoided by the multinational bank since its involvement in foreign nations is confined to the provision of financial services. Similar applications of internalization theory can be made in a regional context, for example to explain the entry of new banks to the California market, see Tschoegl (1980).

The multinational bank also does better than a domestic bank. The latter is confined within a national currency area and is subject to the systematic risk of that economy. Opportunities for internalization are confined by the limited size of the domestic financial sector. Exogenous government regulations may constrain the scope of financial intermediation by domestic banks. In contrast, the multinational bank can escape the specific risks and national banking regulations of any single nation. It can benefit from international diversification and engage in internalization to an extent denied the domestic bank. The process of international financial intermediation by multinational banks is efficient and their performance will reflect this efficiency.

Finally, it is apparent that there are world welfare gains arising from the extent of multinational banking activity. It has long been held, in a domestic context, that financial intermediation helps to improve the efficiency of an economy and stimulates its development. Greater specialization is possible and the improved division of labour increases performance and net output for a nation. Similarly, on an international level, the same welfare gains will be available. The multinational bank is a vehicle for the international division of labour. It cannot maximize world welfare by itself, but it can assist this objective.

The rise of multinational banks should also increase the degree of integration of world capital markets and help to improve their efficiency. The international financial markets and multinational banks are now inexorably intertwined. The theoretical rationale of the multi-national enterprise, namely internalization, can be applied to explain the activities of the multinational bank. For these reasons the relationship between internalization and international banking is likely to become an important subject for more detailed theoretical and empirical analysis in the future.

The approach of this chapter should be contrasted with that of Kotz (1978). He argues that the largest US multinational banks control both US based multinational enterprises and domestic US firms. This control is exercised by the allocation of supplies of capital, by equity stakes in the corporations and by interlocking directorships between the boards of banks and corporations. It would seem that Kotz confuses control with information. Both banks and multinational banks are specialists in the compilation, processing and distribution of information, especially financial information. They supply financial services which have less risk than those available in the market for goods, that is, the banks evaluate the risks and returns of various enterprises as if they (the banks) were individual investors. Banks also supply finance capital to enterprises for specific projects. Yet none of these activities gives the multinational bank control over the production methods of an enterprise. Nor would multinational banks wish to dissipate their scarce managerial energies by attempting to become as knowledgeable as the managers of the enterprise about the industry or firm specific factors affecting individual firms. The relative advantage of banks is in financial inform-ation and the relative advantage of multinational banks is in their ability to react to imperfections in international financial markets. Neither banks nor multinational banks wish to enter the goods market.

The chapter now proceeds to test the benefits of multinational banking. Attention is directed towards the five largest Canadian banks as a somewhat neglected, but still representative, group of multinational banks. Analysis of US banks has been performed in Rugman (1979) where it is found that the earnings of US banks in the period 1965-74 are not excessive but are more stable than the earnings of any other industry examined. Dean and Grubel (1979) have compared the multi-nationality of Canadian and US banks.

Profitability in US and Canadian Banking

There has been a tremendous expansion of Canadian chartered bank involvement in foreign currency banking in the last 20 years and this presents itself as an interesting case study of multinational banking in general. This section discusses some recent work on the profitability of Canadian versus US banking. The following section examines the relation-ship between the increasing degree of multinationality of Canadian banks and the greater expected return for any risk class resulting from the benefits of international diversification. Mintz (1979) has explored the rates of return for Canadian chartered banks between 1963 and 1973. Unlike Rugman (1979), who examines variability of earnings as well as return, Mintz concentrates on return alone. He has two controversial findings.

First, Mintz shows that the rate of return to capital increased significantly after the Bank Act revision of 1967. In the period 1968-73 the return to banks was both absolutely and relatively greater than the return of trust and loan companies, and also of non-financial corporations. Mintz states that the increased profits of the banks are due to favourable interest rate spreads on their domestic operations. Another explanation is that improved returns are due to the greater volume of foreign business activity of the Canadian banks, especially in the new and rapidly expanding Eurocurrency market.

Secondly, Mintz finds significant differences in earnings between Canadian and US banks (of similar size). Rates of return on capital, both before and after taxes, are higher for Canadian banks. These higher profits are needed, says Mintz, since the costs of financial intermediation are greater in Canada than in the United States. The results need to be interpreted cautiously as Mintz makes adjustments in the returns to allow for his interpretation of the different bank regulatory systems in the two nations.

Mintz argues that Canadian banks earned excess profits of from $200 million to nearly $500 million in some of the years in the 1968-73 period, when there was a lack of competition from the domestic financial intermediaries, as well as an effective barrier to foreign entry. Recently these barriers have been less effective and competition from trust and loan companies has increased notably. Mintz's empirical results on rates of return should be contrasted with those of Allen and Giddy (1979) in a study for the US Comptroller of the Currency. Using a more fully-specified theoretical model of the welfare costs of banking regulation, in contrast to the *ad hoc* approach of Mintz, these authors find relatively little difference between the performance of Canadian and US banks.

Another problem with Mintz's work is that he completely ignores the international dimension of Canadian banking. Over the period of his study, the Canadian banking industry became more involved in foreign operations, from some 20 per cent in 1968 up to nearly 30 per cent of total assets by the end of 1973 (as is discussed below with reference to Table 5.1). Mintz neglects both the size of this international influence, and the increasing degree of foreign activities. Therefore his work does not test the hypothesis of international diversification in relation to alternative hypothesis, such as the uncompetitive nature of Canadian banking, or its relatively large scale, over this period. This neglect of the multinational nature of Canadian banking is remedied in the next section of this chapter.

Canadian Banking Goes Multinational

In this section data on the multinational nature of Canadian banking are presented; in the next, level and variability of bank earnings are examined over time. This procedure gives some tentative support to the hypothesis of stable earnings due to international operations and demonstrates that more detailed empirical work is required in the future.

The proposition advanced in the prior theoretical sections is that multinational banks have more stable earnings than domestic banks. By multinational bank is meant one which has a significant proportion of its assets in branches or offices abroad, say a ratio of 20 per cent or more of foreign to total assets. By domestic bank is meant one with little or no foreign assets or earnings. It is not necessary to distinguish between foreign assets being earned by financing the operations of exporters or other traders relative to the assets earned through foreign branches. Both types of foreign activity add to the international dimension of multinational banking.

A full investigation of the performance of multinational banks should attempt to distinguish between various alternative hypotheses about the reasons for such performance. Such theoretical analyses are attempted in Galbraith (1970), Grubel (1977b), Dean and Grubel (1979), Khoury (1980) and Tschoegl (1980), all of whom have different models of the growth of international banking. Thus, the hypothesis of more stable earnings being due to international diversification should be tested against other hypotheses which allege that banks have greater earnings for any level of risk (that is excess profit) due to either large scale or an uncompetitive environment. Unfortunately, all three elements are present in multinational banks, so it is difficult to disentangle them.

The argument that banks go international to follow the multinational enterprise is clearly a subset of the theory of internalization, since the need for a multinational bank to exist to service the multinational enterprise would not arise in a world of perfect capital markets. Galbraith (1970) has argued that much of the growth of foreign currency banking by the Canadian banks represents the taking of a larger share of the world's business in international money. This is a process of internationalization (rather than internalization as analyzed here). Galbraith has also predicted elsewhere that the Canadian banks will continue to go international in the 1980s as they move into host countries to acquire a share of the banking business in those foreign markets. It is possible that the entry may come in the United States, Western Europe and elsewhere.

Table 5.1 reveals that the Canadian chartered banks have become increasingly multinational over the last two-and-a-half decades. Foreign currency assets as a proportion of total assets have risen from 9 per cent in 1955 to some 15 per cent in 1959 and were up to 36 per cent in 1979. As is well known, Canadian banks are very active in the Caribbean, yet during the 1970s the proportion of their foreign currency assets in this area actually failed to grow as rapidly as those in other areas, see Dean and Grubel (1979). Total foreign currency assets grew at a compounded annual growth rate of 18 per cent over this period, from some $1.1 billion[1] in 1955 up to $80.1 billion in 1979. Over the same period domestic assets only grew at an annual compounded rate of 10.5 per cent, from $11.5 billion in 1955 to $141.5 billion by 1979. In the last few years since 1972, the compounded annual growth rate in foreign currency assets is 24 per cent compared to 17 per cent for domestic assets.

Data at firm level, from annual reports of the last ten years or so,

**Table 5.1: The Degree of Multinationality in Canadian Banking
(Canadian Chartered Bank Assets, Per Cent Distribution)**

	Domestic	Foreign
1979	0.64	0.36
1978	0.65	0.35
1977	0.68	0.32
1976	0.70	0.30
1975	0.71	0.29
1974	0.71	0.29
1973	0.71	0.29
1972	0.74	0.26
1971	0.73	0.27
1970	0.71	0.29
1969	0.73	0.27
1968	0.79	0.21
1967	0.80	0.20
1966	0.80	0.20
1965	0.81	0.19
1964	0.78	0.22
1963	0.81	0.19
1962	0.81	0.19
1961	0.82	0.18
1960	0.84	0.16
1959	0.85	0.15

Source: Various issues of the Bank of Canada, *Monthly Review.*

provide information for individual banks on the split between foreign
and domestic assets. Of the five largest chartered banks which account
for virtually all of Canadian banking activity, the Royal Bank has
maintained about a one-third ratio of foreign to total assets over the
1970s, while there is some indication that each of the other banks has
increased this ratio, given the limited periods for which data are available.
The degree of multinationality varies from some 25 per cent for the
Commerce Bank to over 50 per cent for the Bank of Nova Scotia, but
for all banks it has been increasing in recent years.

Dr Jack Galbraith has pointed out to me that a large proportion of
the growth in foreign currency operations of the Canadian chartered
banks is the result of booking foreign currency assets and liabilities in
Canada, rather than the actual growth of foreign branches. He asks

whether a multinational enterprise is an organization that either does business in more than two different countries by transforming inputs into outputs in those countries or whether it is simply buying inputs in different countries, transforming them into outputs in the home nation and then selling the output abroad (that is exporting). Galbraith argues that large Canadian banks do both activities and, while he agrees that the first method of operating foreign branches represents an international diversification of the banking business, he doubts if the second method of banking (mainly US) foreign currency assets in Canada really represents such diversification. Yet in terms of my analysis it does, since the Canadian banks are thereby exposed to an international line of business, rather than confined to lines of business denominated in the domestic currency unit. Export activities are just as good as foreign direct operations in securing offsetting covariances and the resulting benefits of international currency diversification. It is only by gaining access to foreign lines of business that the constraints of regulation of the domestic banking system can be bypassed through internalization.

Performance in Canadian Banking

The rate of return on equity for the five largest Canadian chartered banks is reported in Table 5.2. Profits are the after-tax net income divided by the value of stockholders' equity. This table updates previous work published in Rugman (1979), Chapter 12. To test the proposition that multinational banks have more stable earnings, or greater profit rates for any level of risk, the data on profits can be manipulated to find the means and standard deviations of earnings over time. These are reported in the next table.

Table 5.3 reveals that over the period 1962-79 the average profits of the five banks have been 10.86 per cent, which is close to the average earnings of all corporations in Canada. The standard deviations range from 2.04 to 3.80 (and average 2.8 per cent for all five banks). They are thus considerably lower than those for other industrial sectors in Canada, revealing the relatively stable nature of earnings for Canadian banks.

To test the proposition that earnings have increased as the degree of multinationality rises, Table 5.3 also reports earnings for various sub-periods. The sub-periods are each of six years; the period before the 1967 Bank Act Revision and two periods after it. It has been shown previously (in Table 5.1) that over this 18-year period the degree of

Table 5.2: Canadian Banks' Rates of Return on Equity, Per Cent, 1962-79

	Royal	CIBC	B of M	BNS	T-D
1979	12.3	17.9	17.0	10.7	14.3
1978	12.7	16.9	16.5	11.8	13.5
1977	11.6	17.0	14.6	11.4	12.2
1976	12.6	17.3	14.0	11.4	12.5
1975	13.5	16.4	18.0	13.6	13.5
1974	12.0	12.2	11.2	11.0	14.4
1973	11.8	11.1	14.6	11.2	12.0
1972	11.6	10.7	14.6	11.5	12.9
1971	10.8	9.6	11.2	11.3	12.2
1970	11.4	10.8	11.8	9.4	11.7
1969	10.8	10.3	11.8	10.5	11.6
1968	9.8	9.5	7.7	9.6	10.3
1967	8.7	8.0	8.8	8.3	9.1
1966	8.1	7.7	8.6	7.8	8.4
1965	7.0	7.5	8.3	7.2	7.9
1964	7.3	7.7	8.1	6.9	7.4
1963	7.1	7.5	7.8	6.3	7.3
1962	6.9	7.3	7.5	7.1	7.2

Source: Various Annual Reports of the banks indicated and *The Financial Post* Card Service.

multinationality increased. The data in Table 5.3 reveal that mean profits increased for each bank over each of the three sub-periods, from just under 8 per cent in 1962-7, to over 12 per cent in 1974-9. The risk of earnings has not increased in the same proportions for Royal Bank, Nova Scotia and Toronto-Dominion, while the higher variability in earnings of the Commerce and Bank of Montreal has been compensated by mean profits of 16.3 and 15.2 per cent respectively over the last sub-period.

Unfortunately, it cannot be shown, at this stage, that the increased earnings of Canadian banks are solely due to the advent of multinational-ization. Over the 1962-79 period the Canadian trust and insurance companies, and credit unions, increased in importance on the domestic scene, during the second half of the 1970s. Yet excess profits do not appear to exist. The reasons for the interesting findings of Table 5.4 are still open to question; all that is attempted here is to add the

Table 5.3: Earnings of Leading Canadian Banks Mean and Standard Deviation of Profits, 1967-79 (Per Cent)

	Royal		CIBC		B of M		BNS		T-D	
	Mean	SD	Mean	SD	Mean	SD	Mean	SD	Mean	SD
Total Period										
1962-79	10.3	2.17	11.4	3.80	11.8	3.44	9.8	2.04	11.0	2.44
Sub-periods (6 years)										
1974-9	12.5	0.60	16.3	1.88	15.2	2.26	11.7	0.94	13.4	0.82
1968-73	11.0	0.67	10.3	0.60	12.0	2.34	10.6	0.83	11.8	0.79
1962-7	7.5	0.66	7.6	0.22	8.2	0.45	7.3	0.64	7.9	0.68

Source: As for Table 5.2.

Table 5.4: Leading Canadian Chartered Banks, Rate of Return on Average Assets, Per Cent

| | International | | | | | Domestic | | | | |
	Royal	CIBC	B of M	BNS	T-D	Royal	CIBC	B of M	BNS	T-D
1979	0.67		0.68	0.69	0.64	0.54		0.64	0.78	0.61
1978	0.64		0.72	0.66	0.47	0.62		0.68	0.71	0.70
1977	0.55		0.68	0.67	0.45	0.52		0.50	0.64	0.64
1976	0.54	0.46	0.60	0.59	0.43	0.60	0.64	0.46	0.66	0.71
1975	0.64	0.44	0.48	0.60	0.51	0.66	0.71	0.59	0.58	0.80
1974	0.47	0.22			0.51	0.56	0.68			0.73
1973	0.48	0.23			0.43	0.71	0.74			0.71
1972	0.51	0.24			0.41[a]	0.73	0.75			0.67[a]
1971	0.60	0.08			0.43[a]	0.64	0.68			0.62[a]
1970		0.19			0.29[a]		0.81			0.54[a]
Mean	0.57	0.27	0.63	0.64	0.46	0.62	0.72	0.57	0.67	0.67
SD	0.07	0.13	0.09	0.04	0.09	0.07	0.05	0.08	0.07	0.07

Note: a. Calculated as net revenue after taxes divided by average assets which are calculated as the average of the year-beginning and year-ending levels.
Source: Annual Reports of the respective chartered banks from 1967 to 1979.

multinational dimension of Canadian banking, and its change in time, into the debate. If Canadian banks are oligopolistic, as argued by Dean and Schwindt (1976) and Mintz (1979) then they are also multinational. Both multinational enterprises and multinational banks often have these elements in their make up.

Preliminary work on the bank level difference in earnings on foreign and domestic operations is reported in Tables 5.4 and 5.5. The data provided by each of the five Canadian chartered banks (in their annual reports) are incomplete, making cross comparisons hazardous. However, it is clear that for all of the banks, there is some increase in the profitability of foreign operations in the last few years. In the past, domestic returns on assets had exceeded foreign returns for all of the banks, as demonstrated in Table 5.5. Yet in the last few years the Bank of Montreal has found its foreign operations to be more profitable than domestic ones, while the Royal Bank and Bank of Nova Scotia have almost no differential between foreign and domestic earnings. The data for the Commerce Bank indicate some decrease in the greater profitability of domestic earnings, but the data are incomplete for the most recent years. Only for Toronto-Dominion have domestic earnings remained

Table 5.5: Differentials between Chartered Bank Rates of Return on Domestic and Foreign Currency Assets

	Royal	CIBC	B of M	BNS	T-D
1979	-0.13		-0.04	0.09	-0.03
1978	-0.02		-0.04	0.05	0.23
1977	-0.03		-0.18	-0.03	0.19
1976	0.06	0.18	-0.14	0.07	0.28
1975	0.02	0.27	0.11	-0.02	0.29
1974	0.09	0.46			0.22
1973	0.23	0.51			0.28
1972	0.22	0.51			0.26
1971	0.04	0.60			0.19
1970		0.62			0.25

consistently greater than foreign. There are too few observations (and those that appear in Table 5.4 are inconsistent between banks) to permit a valid measurement of variability of return over time periods.

Table 5.6 provides some extra evidence that, in 1970-5 period, the earnings on domestic operations were greater than on foreign, but that this differential narrowed considerably. In this table returns are found on a pre-tax basis (in contrast to all other tables reported here).

Table 5.6: Domestic and International Business: Five Largest Canadian Banks, 1970-5

	Balance of Revenue as a Percentage of Assets		
	(1) Domestic	(2) International	(3) Differential (1)-(2)
1975	1.35	1.05	0.30
1974	1.18	0.74	0.44
1973	1.34	0.72	0.62
1972	1.35	0.80	0.55
1971	1.29	0.78	0.51
1970	1.45	0.66	0.79

Source: *Report of the Royal Commission on Corporate Concentration* (Ottawa, Ont., March 1978), Table 10-3.

Conclusion

The empirical evidence gathered here, although somewhat scanty, provides some support for the hypothesis that the increasing degree of multinationality in Canadian banking is positively related to earnings. It was found that profits for the largest five Canadian banks have increased in more recent years, at a time when they became more multinational. Yet the increased profits were not due to an increase in domestic profits (since Tables 5.4 and 5.5 reveal that the differential between domestic and foreign earnings fell for all the banks over the last 15 years or so). Instead, the increased mean profit rate in banking is due to greater profits from the foreign operations of Canadian banks. As the extent of multinationality has increased the performance of Canadian banks has improved. Greater return for any level of risk has been observed, but the data are so far inadequate to confirm that there is less risk in earnings (for any level of return) due to the multinational activities of Canadian banks.

The theory of internalization indicates that multinational banks have internal advantages over domestic banks. Some of these advantages are due to the gains from international diversification. Here it has been observed that a group of Canadian banks has increased their profitability as the extent of multinationality grew over the last 25 years. The increase in profits is probably not unrelated to the increase in multi-nationality. Multinational banks therefore seem to be explained by the same process as multinational enterprises. Both banks and corporations experience improved performance as the degree of multinationality increases, a result predicted by the theory of internalization.

Note

1. That is US billions (thousand millions) here and elsewhere.

6 INTERNALIZATION AND THE TRANSFER OF TECHNOLOGY

Introduction

This chapter has as its focus the global strategies of the multinational enterprises (MNEs) as they affect the transfer of technology to host nations, such as Canada. Since these global strategies are determined at the head office by the US parent firm it is necessary to recognize internalization as a generalized theoretical model of the MNE, or at least to appreciate that such a theoretical perspective is available, before engaging in either theoretical or empirical analysis of technology transfer in Canada. A study of research and development (R and D) which ignores the global strategy of the MNE is like Hamlet without the Prince of Denmark.

It has been demonstrated earlier that the activities of MNEs are explained by the theory of internalization. It is a general theory of foreign direct investment and it can be used to explain the methods by which MNEs choose to service foreign markets, namely the choice over time between exporting, foreign direct investment or licensing. Here the theory of internalization is applied to the specific policy issue of technology transfer to Canada. The theory may help to explain why there is little indigenous R and D in Canada, why the MNE has a propensity to prefer foreign direct investment to licensing in Canada and why Canadian technology lags behind that of the United States, Japan and Europe.

In this chapter the theory of internalization is utilized to explain the nature of the transfer of technology to advanced nations (such as Canada) by multinational enterprises and to examine the issue of public policy towards R and D by multinationals. The internal market of the MNE is a mechanism by which it monitors the use of its firm specific advantage in knowledge. Internalization is a superior device to licensing or joint ventures from the viewpoint of the MNE, as the risk of dissipation of its firm specific advantage is minimized. The prediction of internalization theory tested here is the one which states that the MNE will use foreign direct investment (i.e. production by wholly controlled subsidiaries) to minimize the risk of dissipation of its firm specific advantage in knowledge (broadly defined to include technology and/or management skills). Clearly the MNE is not in business to transfer technology to nation states or to otherwise intervene in their affairs *per se*, but it is here to make profits over time, a market test which requires the cautious use of resources and technology by the firm. We shall see that the lack of technological independence by Canada is not the fault of the MNE but is determined by inappropriate Canadian industrial and science policy.

It is obvious that internalization, which is a response to externalities in the pricing of proprietary information, knowledge and intangible management skills occurs when its benefits outweigh the costs. Yet it is an error to confine internalization to these market imperfections alone. Indeed there is no reason why internalization is a theory of *international* production in such a case. To add the missing dimension we need to accept the point that multinational enterprises embody within themselves firm specific advantages which can be maintained only by foreign direct investment (FDI), rather than by such alternative modalities of servicing foreign markets as exporting or licensing. Thus internalization hypothesises that FDI is superior to these other modes because of its lower relative cost. Exporting is also denied by tariffs and licensing faces the risk of dissipation of the firm specific advantage.

A second point is that market imperfections may well be created by government regulations and controls. Internalization is a response to such 'unnatural' market imperfections. Again, recognition of these elements makes internalization into a theory of the multinational enterprise (rather than a domestic firm). Centralization of R and D is an implication of this modern version of the theory of the MNE. Unless the R and D is centralized in the parent there is no firm specific advantage at risk through licensing, yet we know the MNEs prefer to control the rate of use of their knowledge advantage by FDI, thus they must be afraid of dissipation. The consequences of government intervention are to distort the exporting/licensing/FDI choice. We find that if the theory of internalization tells us anything it is that internalization occurs in response to government actions and not independently of such regulations.

Studies on Transfer of Technology, R and D and Knowledge Advantage

Ronstadt (1977) undertook seven case studies of R and D developed in the foreign subsidiaries of US multinationals. He found that the percentage of foreign to total R and D was 9 for Corning, 12 for Union Carbide's Chemicals and Plastics, 23 for Exxon Chemical, 24 for Exxon

Energy, 31 for IBM, 39 for CPC and 45 for Otis Elevator. The main reason for the creation of R and D abroad was to assist in the transfer of technology from the parent to the subsidiary. It is not at all clear that the foreign subsidiaries have an independent R and D capability since their performance in the R and D function is determined by the global strategy of the multinational enterprise. It appears that some subsidiaries of MNEs are allocated R and D tasks of a fragmentary nature, but these are integrated by the parent. It is rare to find a truly independent R and D function performed in a subsidiary.

Teece (1976) examines the cost of technology transfer for 26 projects. He assumes that the US parent has a firm specific advantage in proprietary knowledge. Teece finds that the marginal cost to the MNE of using its knowledge advantage abroad is not zero. Yet economic theory would imply that since knowledge is a public good its price should be zero. Only the theory of internalization shows that the MNE needs to recoup its private costs of R and D by controlling the market for its firm specific advantage. The management fees and other charges identified by Teece as knowledge costs are actually the costs of running an internal market by the MNE. By including what are really actual production and operating costs in his estimates Teece exaggerates his figures. Internalization theory indicates that the MNE can charge reasonable fees for the use of its knowledge advantage by a subsidiary. Licence fees will be even higher than fees to subsidiaries since there is a risk of dissipation of the knowledge advantage by this mode of servicing a foreign market.

Telesio (1979) is one of the first studies to consider licensing as an alternative to subsidiary production by the MNE as a method of servicing foreign markets. Based on his Harvard Business School Dissertation (supervised by Bob Stobaugh), Telesio's work is one of the first efforts at adding an empirical aspect to the mainly theoretical work on alternatives to the MNE. He says that there are two motives for licensing. First, to substitute for FDI when there are restrictions on entry of the MNE making net costs too high. Secondly, for reciprocal exchanges of licences. The latter occurs characteristically in the areas of semiconductor and pharmaceutical technologies. Here interlocking patents are common.

Telesio finds also that there is a gain from trade in licensing. The MNE gains access to valuable assets of the licensee, such as its familiarity with the local market and culture, not to mention the avoidance of political risk and regulations on FDI itself. In exchange the MNE surrenders its proprietary rights over certain firm specific advantages such as knowledge. Thus, by licensing there is always a risk of dissipation of the MNE's secret technology. Telesio also finds that little licensing is done with developing countries relative to the large amount with advanced nations.

Telesio hypothesizes that five variables affect the evaluation of the net benefits of licensing to the MNE. These are: the firm's internal supply of proprietary knowledge, its degree of product diversification, its size relative to other firms in its main industry, its experience of foreign markets and the degree of technological competition. A sample of 66 MNEs (mainly US based) is used to test the hypotheses. In some of the regressions the dependent variable is a dummy variable, equal to one for reciprocal licensing, and zero if the firm does not license technology reciprocally. The five independent variables are: the ratio of R and D to sales, size, degree of product diversification, sales of subsidiaries and nationality of the MNE. For firms that use licensing as an alternative to FDI it is found that licensing is positively related to amount of R and D from sales, extent of product diversification, relatively small or medium size, inexperience in foreign operations as proxied by extent of FDI and degree of competition. In some tests (Chapter 4) only R and D and product diversification are significant independent variables in regressions for firms that license for reciprocal access to technology. In other tests of reciprocal licensing (in Chapter 6) R and D and competition are found to be insignificant. Large size is related to degree of licensing, as is diversification and lack of foreign experience. While the work is beset by small sample problems, these results are provocative.

Vernon and Davidson (1979) examine the worldwide spread of innovation by US based multinationals. They find that the research intensive MNEs produce abroad rather than engage in licensing, subject to the qualification that the internal organization of some firms, notably global product firms, leads to a preference for licensing over subsidiary production. They also find that the interval between US innovation and the first use of the technology overseas has been shrinking in the post-war period, and that MNEs set up new product lines more speedily in their subsidiaries abroad. Firms still face information costs about foreign markets, so they prefer to produce in familiar foreign locations and to concentrate on extending overseas production of a product line already developed at home. There is, however, some limited evidence of a trend towards greater diversity in products made abroad, and in geographical areas, from the more familiar areas of Canada and Latin America towards Europe, Asia and even Africa.

These findings are based on one data set for all the foreign subsidiaries of 180 US based MNEs over the 1965-75 period. Another data set confined to new product data is also used. This consists of the 406 innovations introduced by 57 US MNEs after 1945, and includes the spread of licensees as well as subsidiaries. In addition 548 imitations introduced by these MNEs are recorded. Data on numbers of foreign subsidiaries and timing of establishment, available in Vaupel and Curhan (1969), is also used. Prachowny and Richardson (1975), Hewitt (1980a) and other researchers, have made use of some of these data from the Harvard multinational enterprise project. In particular use has been made of data which identify the average age of subsidiaries and their structure. The jury is still out on this evidence and its relationship to the determinants of R and D in parents and subsidiaries.

Given this caveat it can still be concluded that the available evidence appears to support internalization theory. When Vernon and Davidson find that research intensive MNEs tend to produce abroad rather than license it is due to the prediction of internalization theory that states that the MNE has a firm specific advantage which is at risk unless it is protected within the firm's internal market. Licensing faces the risk of dissipation of the knowledge advantage. Therefore MNEs (which are characterized as enjoying high R and D activities) have advantages in proprietary information which are best defended by the controlled production of foreign affiliates rather than by licensing.

The Transfer of Technology to Canada

Canada is a small, open economy dominated by multinational corporations. Although the nation enjoys one of the highest standards of living in the world many groups have questioned its lack of technological independence. Canada does only half the R and D of the United States. It has been well documented that the ratio of R and D expenditures to GNP for Canada is under 1 per cent, while it is over 2 per cent for the United States (in 1975 the figures were 1.0 and 2.4 respectively). Most advanced European nations have a percentage tending more towards two than one while the United States' percentage has historically been close to three. Indeed Canada seems to have one of the lowest percentages of all advanced nations. Furthermore, the ratio has fallen from an average of 1.2 in the 1960s to just below 1 per cent in recent years.

It has been advocated by the Science Council of Canada, and by various nationalist groups, that Canada should seek to increase the ratio of R and D to GNP. One fashionable method is to pursue a 'world product mandate' under which Canadian based multinational firms would generate technology at home for future export abroad. The viability of such a policy of sectoral self sufficiency in technology is explored here. The objective of the production of technology is also related to the objective of consumption and income generation for the nation as a whole.

Data for 1977 by the Ministry of State for Science and Technology (MOSST) demonstrate that private business enterprises generate 44 per cent of R and D in Canada, while the Universities account for 24.4 per cent and the Government 31.4 per cent. The private sector's share had increased from 38.7 per cent in 1963 and 41.6 per cent in 1971. This performance by private firms is good, considering that they spend relatively less in generating R and D (34.9 per cent in 1977) than does the government sector (48.3 per cent). In addition, the Universities spend only 11.8 per cent, but their share in effective output of R and D is twice this figure, i.e. the 24.4 per cent mentioned in the first sentence of this paragraph. In other industrialized nations the business sector is the source of 40 to 50 per cent of R and D, and performs 50 to 65 per cent of R and D. This is assumed by MOSST to imply that Canadian industry is inefficient in the generation of R and D.

The Science Council of Canada (1979) and two of their most influential researchers, Britton and Gilmour (1978), have advanced a strategy of technological independence for Canada. They advocate such a nationalistic policy since they believe that there is insufficient transfer of technology to Canada from the multinational enterprises which dominate the nation. Nor is there an attractive climate for indigenous innovation in an economy with truncated firms, high production costs, low relative productivity and excessive concentration.

The preference of the Science Council for technological sovereignty has been roundly criticized by Daly (1979) and Safarian (1979). Using basic economic analysis these authors demonstrate that there are internal inconsistencies in the Science Council's analysis. They also find that a nationalist science policy (like the tariff) is inefficient. They conclude that government intervention to support domestic technology would not be successful in sustaining domestic technological development.

Martin *et al.* (1979) have discovered that there are substantial differences in the speed and adaption of innovations by provinces in Canada. The Economic Council of Canada examined the regional diffusion of innovation in several industries, namely computers, electric furnaces in steel, roof trusses in construction, ocean containers, newsprint presses and shopping centres. They find that the regional diffusion of innovation reveals significant and systematic lags. In turn, such lags help to explain the differences in productivity across provinces and the persistence of regional income disparities.

R and D, Technology Transfer and Foreign Ownership in Canada

The relationship between R and D, degree of foreign control of manufacturing industry and extent of export activity has been studied most recently by Bones (1980). His analysis of Statistics Canada industry level data reveals that most R and D in Canada is done by multinational firms. In 1975 more than 80 per cent of R and D by all Canadian industries took place in seven manufacturing industries, namely aircraft and parts, electrical products, petroleum, machinery, chemicals, primary metals and paper.

These research-intensive industries undertake 85 per cent of R and D in manufacturing although they only account for 40 per cent of value added in Canadian manufacturing. In these seven research-intensive manufacturing industries there occurs the highest degree of foreign ownership. The percentage of foreign control of industry sales (shown in parentheses) is: aircraft and parts (82.7), electrical (65.6), petroleum (96.0), machinery (67.5), chemicals (82.9), primary metals (17.1) and paper (43.6).

Thus it can be confirmed that the great bulk of R and D generated in Canada takes place in the manufacturing industries which experience the highest degree of foreign control. Translating this finding to a firm level analysis implies that the subsidiaries of (mainly US) multinational firms active in Canada are responsible for R and D. In turn, this implies that Canadian public policy towards R and D must start from the premise that multinational firms dominate the R and D component of the manufacturing sector of the economy.

In a more speculative part of the paper, Bones argues that the R and D expenditures of foreign controlled firms are about the same amount as those of Canadian controlled firms. Unadjusted Statistics Canada data for 1975 reveal that the R and D expenditures are higher (relative to sales) for Canadian controlled manufacturing firms than for foreign controlled firms. Yet Bones demonstrates that the R and D expenditures by foreign controlled firms exclude payments for technology and knowledge made to non-residents (i.e. to the parent company). For example, excluded are payments for patents, industrial designs, scientific and research services, royalties and other fees for technology related services. If these payments are added to R and D expenditures of foreign controlled manufacturing firms there is no divergence between the R and D of Canadian and foreign controlled firms. Similar findings were made in the study by Safarian (1966).

Bones also examines the relationship between export performance of research-intensive Canadian and foreign controlled firms. In the most research-intensive Canadian manufacturing industries Bones finds that, in 1970, foreign controlled firms accounted for only 35 per cent of exports although they were responsible for 75 per cent of sales. Bones attributes the poor export performance of research-intensive, foreign owned manufacturing firms to the excessively diversified product lines and small size of the Canadian economy. These and related factors prevent the development of a home market base upon which exporting can be built. Presumably Bones also means to argue (although he is not explicit) that these factors affect foreign controlled manufacturing firms much more than they affect Canadian controlled firms. To this I would add the observation that multinationals in Canada are generally found in import competing sectors, so they should not be expected to be very good at exporting.

Frankl (1979), in a new econometric analysis for IT&C, finds a strong positive relationship between R and D intensity in Canadian industries and their US counterparts. There is a significant negative relationship between the degree of foreign control and the difference between Canadian and US R and D intensities. Size of firm is not found to be significant. It is also reported that: 'R and D intensity levels were generally greater in the Canadian controlled segments of industries than in the foreign controlled segments' (p. 52).

These results confirm the theory of internalization, which predicts that R and D originates in the home country of the multinational firm, rather than in the host nation. Frankl suggests that the parent multinational will enjoy scale economies in R and D, and also benefit from indivisibilities in R and D. The Canadian subsidiary will experience truncation of its R and D capacity. She also suggests that the results support a second hypothesis, namely 'that there are greater barriers to technology flow between independent firms than between affiliates'. The regressions from which these results emerge were run on a data base for 110 Canadian manufacturing industries and their US counterparts for 1972. The original data base was developed by Robert Owen in a recent Princeton dissertation.

The overall result of the Frankl study is that R and D intensity in

Canadian industry is lower than that in the United States. This poor performance (from the viewpoint of the host nation) is due almost entirely to the extensive foreign control of Canadian industry. Frankl's study thereby confirms the predictions of internalization theory. She argues that R and D expenditures in Canada would almost double if the R and D in Canadian subsidiaries were of the same proportion as R and D expenditures of parent firms.

At a disaggregated level Frankl finds that in aircraft and parts the R and D intensity is significantly greater than expected on the basis of its degree of foreign ownership and technological intensity. This is said to be due to special benefits from government subsidies and defence programmes. Yet another study, of the automotive industry, has the opposite finding. There is significantly less R and D intensity in both the foreign controlled sector and the total automobile industry than was expected. If the R and D intensity of foreign controlled firms in the automotive industry were to increase to equal that of US parent firms, then total R and D expenditures in Canada for all manufacturing industry would increase by 40 per cent.

To summarize, these two recent studies support my application of internalization theory in a Canadian context. They confirm that, while foreign owned firms in Canada engage in most of the R and D, these subsidiaries undertake less R and D than the parent firms. There is mixed evidence as to whether independent Canadian firms do as little R and D as the subsidiaries after allowing for their smaller size.

The Canadian Balance of Payments for Technology

There are several potential indicators of a nation's technological progress. The actual dollar expenditures on R and D to sales have been used by Howe and McFetridge (1976). The ratio of R and D to sales has been studied by Frankl (1979). The number of employees in R and D activities per 1,000 employees has been used by Globerman (1973). Another index of technological progressiveness is the number of inventions per industry, as proxied by the number of patents either registered, or used, per industry. Such data are available in Statistics Canada, *Annual Review of Science Statistics*. However, if internalization theory is applied here, it predicts that relatively few, if any, inventions will take place in Canadian industry, since much of it is foreign owned. Thus another index of technological progressiveness will be the payments made by foreign owned subsidiaries for the use of their parents'

Table 6.1: Canadian Business Payments to Non-residents for Technology Transfers, 1970-7 ($ Millions)

All industries payment type	1970	1971	1972	1973	1974	1975	1976	1977
Dividends	701.8	791.1	868.8	1,023.8	1,278.3	1,433.2	1,360.7	1,454.2
Interest	521.6	523.3	515.5	571.8	712.4	793.6	845.1	928.3
Subtotal	1,223.4	1,314.4	1,384.3	1,595.6	1,990.7	2,226.8	2,205.8	2,382.5
Payments for technology								
(A) Rent	141.4	138.5	141.2	160.8	237.6	274.3	208.8	212.2
(B) Royalties: total	163.7	192.9	221.8	263.2	342.6	408.5	435.2	482.9
– copyrights	18.1	25.3	30.1	48.8	36.3	38.0	50.8	53.1
– patents	32.4	37.1	35.7	38.3	47.8	39.8	48.3	46.5
– industrial designs	39.2	42.2	59.9	57.0	23.4	38.5	31.4	33.2
– trademarks	16.6	15.1	17.7	22.2	28.0	38.4	40.8	50.5
– others	57.4	72.0	78.4	97.0	207.1	263.9	263.9	299.6
(B1) Franchises	51.3	41.4	39.8	23.4	35.1	29.0	37.7	34.6
Royalties and franchises: total	214.8	234.3	261.6	286.6	377.7	437.7	472.9	517.5
(C) Research and development	79.5	79.1	80.4	79.8	84.3	99.6	108.6	132.3
(D) Fees for professional services: total	88.8	149.8	128.4	180.75	230.3	313.3	233.3	259.0
– engineering	77.0	138.4	114.5	167.3	214.9	297.6	214.1	237.3
– others	11.8	11.4	13.9	13.2	15.4	15.7	19.2	21.7
(D1) Management fees	121.0	143.7	132.3	153.1	180.8	240.0	265.9	296.7
All fees: total	209.8	293.5	260.7	333.6	411.1	553.3	499.2	555.7
(E) Others: total	184.3	179.9	164.0	136.0	144.2	115.9	241.0	293.0
– advertsing	33.1	42.5	34.5	25.7	27.0	30.1	28.8	30.6
– insurance	19.4	17.4	20.3	21.0	23.3	20.7	23.9	25.5
– remunerations of officers	18.3	18.9	28.0	18.7	20.7	21.6	20.2	19.3
– annuities, pensions	0.9	1.0	2.4	3.1	1.2	1.5	1.2	1.3
– consulting fees not included above	112.6	100.1	78.8	67.5	72.0	42.0	166.9	216.3
Technology subtotal:[a]	830.3	925.6	907.8	996.9	1,254.9	1,480.8	1,530.6	1,710.8
Total[b]	2,053.4	2,239.3	2,292.1	2,592.4	3,245.6	3,707.5	3,736.5	4,093.3

Notes: a. The total of the subtotals will not always correspond due to rounding.
b. The total figures are as presented in the CALURA reports.
Source: CALURA, i.e. Statistics Canada, *Corporations and Labour Unions Return Act*, annual (Ottawa), various issues 1970-7.

technology. The data on such payments for technology are now analyzed.

Table 6.1 provides information on the Canadian balance of techno-logical payments for the last eight years for which data are available, 1970-7. These data are drawn from the Annual Reports under the Corporations and Labour Unions Returns Act (CALURA). This table breaks total payments to non-residents of Canada into two distinct groups. The first is payments of dividends and interest, which should really be discounted as payments for technology (as discussed above). Secondly, are the true payments for technology, namely royalties, rents, management fees and other R and D related payments. The CALURA data do not permit as good a breakdown as the Science Statistics. Unfortunately, the latter data are available only for 1975.

The figures used for Table 6.1 follow the CALURA method of adding dividends and interest to the true payments for technology. This methodology more than doubles the payments to non-residents for technology from the level of about $1.5 billion identified here for 1976 up to a total of nearly $4 billion. This CALURA approach is misleading, since interest is a payment for portfolio rather than direct investment. Furthermore the dividends paid out for the latter type of investment are not necessarily for the use of technology alone, but are more likely to be proportional to the total sales of subsidiaries. Thus, dividends reflect the size and growth of the total Canadian market rather than the firm specific internal technology transfers of multinationals them-selves. A theoretically precise measure of technological payments is difficult to derive so present accounting practices should be interpreted cautiously.

In the true payments for technology the largest payments are for management and professional fees, followed by royalties where these include payments for patents, industrial design, trademarks and copy-rights. Most of the rents are payments for the rental of machinery. Others include payments for franchises, advertising, insurance and consulting fees. Even these data are deficient since they include items which are not necessarily related to technology transfer, such as copy-right royalties, insurance and advertising.

This table on technological payments is only one side of the equation. On the other are the benefits of technology transfer to Canada as multinational enterprises shift up the nation's aggregate production function. The complex issues of the economic effects of multinationals in Canada are explored at greater length in Rugman (1980b). Here it is only necessary to emphasize that the alleged lack

of R and D in Canada is related directly to the degree of foreign ownership of Canadian industry, which, in turn, is related to the tariff and
other protectionist policies. The issue of technology transfer to Canada
is really a problem of misguided public policy in Canada. The nature
of the multinational enterprise, as explained by internalization theory,
is to respond to market imperfections, such as tariffs. Consequently we
should not expect the MNE to act as an agent for the transfer of technology, to Canada or to any other nation.

Internalization and Technology Transfer

The MNEs have a global strategy in the use of their R and D. They seek
to preserve the knowledge advantage unique to the firm by the process
of internalization. This implies that little innovation or worthwhile R and
D is undertaken in Canada by foreign owned firms, and that independent
Canadian owned firms will do relatively more R and D. The two parts of
this statement are now explained more fully.

First, subsidiaries of US multinationals operating in Canada exist to
increase the net revenues of the parent firms, rather than to stimulate
more Canadian research productivity. The spectre of entropy is a greater
incentive for centralized R and D expenditures by multinational firms
rather than any amount of non-specific government incentive grants
going to their foreign subsidiaries.

Secondly, a redirection of Canadian funding for R and D away
from foreign owned firms and towards more basic research in universities
and research institutions may well increase research productivity. Such
basic research generates property rights in knowledge which can then be
sold to either Canadian (or even foreign firms). A greater supply of
basic research within Canada should, in practice, stimulate the development of more technology intensive Canadian owned firms, which
themselves may become multinationals as they market or produce
abroad products using this new knowledge. The areas of advanced
manufacturing in which Canada should expect to develop a separate
technological capability depend upon other factors such as scale
economies, foreign competition, relative costs of all factor inputs and
so on. Yet, all other things equal, subsidies for R and D should include
more R and D in Canadian owned firms.

At the same time R and D expenditures in truly independent
Canadian firms can be encouraged by selective government incentives
which will stimulate the production and adaptation of new technologies

suitable for the smaller Canadian market. Instead, it is cheaper to adapt and use foreign technology. The overriding concern should be for efficiency rather than a misconceived attempt to achieve technological independence in an integrated world.

Therefore these secondary propositions suggest that MNEs prefer production by subsidiaries to licensing; that a policy of technological sovereignty for Canada is difficult in an interdependent world economy; that the present federal government subsidies for technology development are going to foreign owned subsidiaries as well as domestic firms, with little resulting generation of independent Canadian technology; and that public expenditures on R and D are possibly misplaced in any case since the theory of internalization suggests that innovation comes from the private sector as firms seek to retain their firm specific advantages in knowledge.

More specifically, this chapter will examine data on the relative R and D expenditures of samples of foreign owned subsidiaries versus independent Canadian firms. Using the theory of internalization as a seminal base the empirical analysis tests to see if the R and D expenditures by foreign affiliates are less than those by the parent MNEs. It notes that these R and D expenditures of the MNE need to be contrasted with the special costs of licensing, namely the risk of dissipation of the technology advantage of the MNE.

Related propositions are the following: first, Canadian industry does relatively less R and D, per unit of sales, than does US industry; secondly, subsidiaries of US multinationals do less R and D than Canadian owned firms of the same size in the same industry; thirdly, R and D decisions are made by the parent firm as part of its global strategy for the multinational enterprise; fourthly, the transfer of technology to Canada is done at the firm level, as the multinational expands its firm specific advantage to a wider market; fifthly, Canadian science policy has been misguided since most of the government subsidies for R and D went to foreign owned subsidiaries of US firms, who used the grants to increase profits rather than to generate new R and D.

The chapter now proceeds to examine the recent empirical literature on the determinants of research and development in Canada. This literature is found to offer an inadequate explanation of the motivation for technology transfer to Canada, which takes place at the firm level, rather than at the national level as assumed in the econometric work reviewed here. It is found that an appropriate test of the theory of internalization requires a firm level analysis of relative expenditures on R and D by parent, subsidiary and independent Canadian firms.

The Determinants of R and D in Canada

A consistent finding of recent econometric work on the determinants of R and D in Canada is that the amount of grants for R and D from the federal government is important. Globerman (1973) at industry level, Howe and McFetridge (1976) at firm level for the electrical industry, Hewitt (1980b) at firm level also for the electrical industry, and Alexander (1980) at industry level have all found government financed R and D to be a significant variable positively related to the amount of R and D actually undertaken in Canada. The main elements of these studies are summarized in Table 6.2.

Globerman (1973) finds the ratio of government-financed R and D per dollar of sales over the 1965-9 period is a significant independent variable in his stratified regressions, for a sample of nine technologically progressive industries. Other significant variables are foreign ownership (run as a continuous variable) and concentration ratio, both for 1965. His dependent variable is the ratio of R and D employees per 1,000 employees over the 1965-9 period and the regressions reported are in linear form.

Howe and McFetridge (1976) use firm level data, where R and D expenditures are the dependent variable. The regressions are in linear form and use pooled data to generate twelve dummies for the electrical industry and eight for chemicals. The machinery industry has no dummies. For the electrical industry the significant independent variables (for either foreign or domestically owned firms) are sales, sales squared, sales cubed, profits, depreciation and government incentive grants for R and D. Depreciation charges and the Herfindahl index are insignificant. After adding the two other industry groups studies, chemicals and machinery, none of these independent variables is consistently significant across the three industries; for example, grants are insignificant in both chemicals and machinery.

Hewitt (1980b) uses firm level data to construct a novel dependent variable, the ratio of R and D done by Canadian subsidiaries to the total worldwide R and D of the US parent multinational firms. In the electrical industry the level of government incentive grants, the ratio of parents' worldwide R and D to sales and the percentage of US ownership in the Canadian subsidiaries equity are the significant independent variables. Grants are positively related to Canadian R and D. Unfortunately, in the two other industries studies at firm level, machinery and chemicals, there are no significant independent variables. Therefore Hewitt's results on the grants variable are as poor as those of Howe and

Table 6.2: Summary of the Determinants of R and D

Author	Dependent variable	Functional form time period	Independent variables and sign			
			Foreign ownership	Concentration	Grants	Size
Globerman (1973)	R and D employees per 1000 employees industry level	Linear 1965-9	NS in 15 industries Significant +	NS in 15 industries Significant −	NS in 15 industries Significant +	NS in 15 industries Significant
		9 industries only				
Howe and McFetridge (1976)	R and D expenditures	Linear 1967-71	NA	NS in 2 of 3	Significant +	Significant +
		Electrical only				
Hewitt (1980b)	R and D in Canadian subsidiary as a percentage of worldwide self financed R and D of a US multinational	Mainly log 1975	NS in 2 of 3	NA	NS in 2 of 3	NA
		Electrical only				
Alexander (1980)	R and D expenditures over sales	Linear 1974-7	NS	NS	Significant +	NS

Notes: NA = not applicable. NS = not significant. Significant = significant at the 5 per cent level.

McFetridge, since they also failed to detect significances for this variable in two out of three cases.

Alexander (1980) uses industry level data from CALURA for 1974-7. The dependent variable is the ratio of R and D to sales (although R and D and patents are also used). The only significant independent variable is government grants for R and D, divided by sales. Insignificant variables are: foreign ownership, technological progressiveness, concentration, size (sales) and financial variables such as net profits over equity and depreciation.

At firm level, R and D to sales is positively related to size (of firm) and to concentration ratio, see Scherer (1970). Also the larger firms in Canada tend to secure more patents relative to smaller firms, see McFetridge and Weatherly (1977). At industry level there is a weaker relationship between size and R and D expenditures. Indeed, technological progressiveness is sometimes not related in a significant manner to sales, see Alexander (1980), Hewitt (1980a), although Howe and McFetridge (1976) do find sales variables are significant in the linear determination of absolute R and D expenditures for three industry groups. The disparities are not really very surprising, since industry level data-aggregates the firm level effects, such that size washes out as a variable affecting R and D.

Other variables affect R and D and have been tested in studies of the interrelationship between foreign ownership, tariffs, concentration ratios, etc. Orr (1974) shows that concentration ratios are related to tariffs and other barriers to entry. In turn, some authors find concentration and/or tariffs related to profitability and degree of foreign ownership – see Eastman and Stykolt (1967). These findings are stronger using firm level data, but they also tend to hold across industries.

Safarian (1966) could not find any difference in R and D expenditures between resident and non-resident firms. His results, based on his survey of foreign owned firms in the Canadian economy in the early 1960s, are reported in Chapter 6 of his now classic study. The sample and survey response method of Safarian does not lend itself readily to econometric investigation so his findings cannot be regarded as definitive.

In related research on the structure of Canadian industry several other authors have examined the relationships between size, foreign control and profitability. Bloch (1974) does not find that foreign owned firms, or ones in concentrated industries, earn greater profits than domestic firms. Rosenbluth (1970) finds that foreign controlled firms are larger than domestic ones in the same industry, although Safarian had found no marked difference in size – due mainly to Safarian's deliberate omission of the smaller firms from his survey. Rosenbluth does not 'find that the level of foreign control among the leading firms is correlated with the level of concentration' (p. 23). He finds, on the basis of data for 1964, that there was a trend 'towards a decrease in the relative importance of foreign controlled firms among the leading oligopolists' (p. 28).

Daly (1979) and elsewhere, has examined the Schumpeterian point that there are economies of scale in R and D. Scale economies permit the high fixed costs and overheads of R and D to be spread over large runs. Unfortunately, in Canada the small size of the economy and the effects of protection mean that short runs are characteristic of industry. Daly argues that this helps explain why both Canadian and foreign owned companies undertake relatively little R and D in Canada.

Shapiro (1980) examines the performance of foreign owned versus domestic firms in Canada in a new empirical study which is a welcome addition to the literature of international business in general and of Canadian industrial organization in particular. His book is in the tradition of work by Safarian (1966), Rosenbluth (1970), Bloch (1974) and other specialists on the structure of Canadian industry and foreign ownership.

Using a new data base, Shapiro examines the interrelationships between the key variables affecting a firm's economic performance, such as size of firm, degree of foreign ownership, concentration ratio and growth rate. Shapiro throws new light on previous studies in this area, which have been somewhat indecisive. In addition, he extends the analysis in a significant new direction by giving substantial attention to the financial characteristics of Canadian and foreign owned firms. Here he builds upon the work of Pattison (1978) for Canada, and that of Robbins and Stobaugh (1973) on other countries and for multinational firms. Shapiro's integration of economic theory and financial analysis is more comprehensive than much of the previous work done in this area. He uses the Hymer-Caves approach to multinational firms and identifies the internal market of multinationals as a firm specific ownership advantage. Thus his work can be regarded as a test of internalization theory.

The main element which distinguishes Shapiro's work is his diligent exploitation of a novel data base. The data are drawn from detailed corporation financial statistics collected for the Corporations and Labour Unions Returns Act (CALURA). While aggregated CALURA data are published by Statistics Canada, Shapiro makes use of new unpublished disaggregated balance sheet information. These CALURA data are used at the three-digit level for the 1968-72 period. The sample includes some

750 large firms in the manufacturing sector with assets of $5 million or more. These large firms account for 75 per cent of all manufacturing assets. The numerous small firms excluded from the study are mainly Canadian owned but the author argues that this is unlikely to bias the results, especially since he is mainly concerned with a comparison of the relative performance of three categories of corporations: US owned, Canadian owned and other foreign owned. Data on some 60 financial and economic items are manipulated to analyze the performance of these three categories of firms.

Canadian controlled firms are found to be slightly smaller than US or other foreign controlled firms, although the difference is not statistically significant when size is measured by assets. Yet measured by sales US controlled firms are significantly larger than Canadian or other foreign controlled firms. The correlation between assets and sales is 0.78 for all firms in the sample. The relatively strong support for the classic relationship between size and foreign control is not matched by support for a similar correlation between foreign control and the concentration ratio. Shapiro does not find significant relationship between US control and high concentration, a result which is somewhat similar to that of Rosenbluth using data of an earlier vintage.

Shapiro finds widespread differences in the financial structure of the three groups of firms. The US controlled firms use retained earnings more than other methods, while other foreign controlled firms have more debt financing. When they do use debt financing US firms borrow mainly from affiliates. In a related study, at a more aggregate level, Pattison found that foreign controlled firms use retained earnings rather than debt, in comparison to Canadian firms; a finding that is apparently biased by the inclusion of US controlled firms along with other foreign controlled firms as one group. Shapiro also finds that while US controlled firms accumulate more inventories than domestic firms they are still efficient in turning over inventories. The US owned firms are not more liquid than other firms once inventories are netted out. They also tend to invest less in affiliated companies than the other foreign and Canadian firms, perhaps due to remittance of funds to their parents.

In his model of the determinants of profitability Shapiro generates significant coefficients for most of his independent variables, yet the explained variation is only about 20 per cent. Variables positively related to profits are: size, size squared, concentration ratio (as measured by the Herfindahl index), foreign control, leverage, turnover ratio and growth. The variance of earnings is usually insignificant (pp. 86-7). Shapiro produces evidence to demonstrate that US owned firms earn higher profits than other firms in Canada. The US firms also have less risk (measured by variance) in their earnings. The higher mean and more stable earnings of US firms hold across several measures of profitability and are probably due to the advantage of internalization. Shapiro does not find that size is positively related to profitability; indeed, across most size classes he says that 'increasing firm size brings with it neither an increase in profit rates, nor a decrease in variability' (p. 75). For Canadian firms profitability declines as size increases. Over the 1968-72 period of the study Shapiro notes that the US-Canadian differential in profitability persisted. Yet, despite their profitability, Shapiro discovers that US controlled firms do not necessarily grow faster than other firms.

Shapiro fails to include two important variables in his work; namely, the tariff and expenditures on R and D. The tariff is excluded due to a lack of detailed data at the three-digit level, but an attempt is made to capture some of the effects of the tariff by the use of dummy variables for 13 industry groupings. The subsequent work reported fails to draw out fully the important implications of the tariff for profitability, concentration and financial performance of the sample firms. Similarly, the fundamental nature of R and D expenditures by parent multinationals and the undetermined impact of such R and D on the relative performance of subsidiaries versus independent domestic firms is not considered, again due to the lack of R and D data at the three-digit level. A little less concern for the virtue of the statistical data set in hand and more interest in the unresolved theoretical issues about the interrelationships between tariffs, foreign ownership, R and D, concentration and other relevant variables would have improved his study. As it stands Shapiro's work is not definitive but it represents a significant advance in the continuing study of the influence of foreign ownership on the structure of Canadian industry.

Firm Level Tests Required to Replace Aggregative Studies

The interdependencies among the key variables affecting the structure of Canadian industry preclude the development of a theory based on causal relationships. Instead all of the following variables are interrelated in some positive manner:

- Tariffs
- Foreign ownership

 — Size
 — Concentration
 — R and D
 — Profitability
 — Growth rate

Many empirical studies, by a generation of Canadian economists, have examined sub-sets of these variables, with somewhat ambiguous results. If anything, these studies identify a positive relationship amongst the seven variables, although there are possible offsetting partial influences between any two variables.

The less than satisfactory outcome of these very detailed and exhaustive analytical studies of the determinants of R and D in Canada is the result of a fundamental misconception. The authors attempt to identify the significant variables determining R and D, where the dependent variable is viewed from a national perspective. Instead the very point of internalization theory is that R and D is determined within the multinational firm. Therefore a firm level analysis is required rather than the economy wide ones which have been undertaken so far.

The existing studies fall down since they have to straddle the artificial constraints of national boundaries. The studies attempt to identify the impact of grants by the Canadian government on R and D expenditures, yet internalization theory predicts that decisions on R and D in Canadian subsidiaries are made by parent multinationals as part of their global investment strategy. Studies of variables which implicitly assume the autonomy of a nation state are not too helpful when the host nation's manufacturing sector is dominated by multinational firms. Therefore studies of technological intensity (as proxied by the ratio of R and D to sales) must be conceived and performed within the context of firm level analysis.

This work makes the assumption that the level of R and D in Canada is explained better by what happens in the headquarters of an American multinational firm rather than by any list of variables drawn from the Canadian economy. The R and D undertaken by subsidiaries of a US multinational operating in Canada is predicated on the global strategy of that multinational enterprise. The actions of the Canadian federal and provincial governments to promote R and D in the nation will enter into the decision making set of the multinational enterprise only on its periphery. Thus, subsidies for R and D are of little importance to the multinational firm when it makes its basic internal decisions regarding ongoing and future firm level R and D expenditures.

Conversely, the expenditures of the Canadian government for R and D will be of great importance to independent Canadian firms. The subsidies will act as an incentive to private industry in Canada and, all other things equal, should generate greater domestic technological innovations. This distinction between foreign and domestic owned firms is basic to Canadian industrial organization since the motivation of the two sets of firms is different. The remainder of this chapter reports on a simple test of the basic implications of internalization theory in a Canadian context.

The Relative Expenditures on Research and Development by Foreign and Domestic Firms in Canada

The remainder of this chapter examines the relative expenditures on research and development (R and D) by three groups of corporations operating in Canada. These are: the parent firms (usually US based multinational enterprises); the Canadian subsidiaries of the multinationals; and a group of independent Canadian owned firms of similar size to the subsidiaries. Due to the absence of published data on the R and D performed by subsidiaries a severely limited sample of firms is studied. In the next section the characteristics of the subsidiary sample are related to those of their parents and a group of Canadian owned firms. Following this there is an explanation of various statistical tests performed on the differences in R and D undertaken by firms in the three samples.

The basic hypothesis examined is that the R and D undertaken by subsidiaries is less than that of independent Canadian firms. In turn, the lack of R and D in subsidiaries is explained by the theory of internalization. As explained above, this new theory states that subsidiaries exist to extend abroad the firm specific advantage of the parent firm and that the multinational enterprises choose to regulate the use of their advantages through an internal market.

There are no published data on the R and D undertaken by subsidiaries of multinational firms operating in Canada. For that matter there is little information available on R and D by independent Canadian firms. All the publicly available Statistics Canada data are at industry level; for example, all data in the CALURA reports and also in the Science Statistics on R and D are for industries.

Two recent academic studies have used firm level data, but the statistics for these studies are not publicly available. For example, Howe

and McFetridge (1976) use corporation tax returns supplied to them
on a confidential basis by the Department of National Revenue, but
these data are no longer available to the independent researcher. Hewitt
(1980b) uses firm level data on R and D supplied by the Education,
Science and Culture Division of Statistics Canada, again on a basis so
confidential that the Division runs the regressions he specifies. The
Department of Industry, Trade and Commerce have some data on R and
D by subsidiaries but this firm level data set is not available nor have any
studies been published which use it. There are tax returns and financial
statistics in agencies of the government of Canada which contain
information on R and D, and other firm level variables, but again these
are not published.

The information used in this project came from a survey of R and D
expenditures made by the *Financial Post* and reported in their issue of
10 June 1978. The survey covered 35 corporations active in R and D in
Canada, as identified by a directory of research establishments compiled
by the Ministry of State for Science and Technology (MOSST). The
Financial Post report data on the 35 corporations in the private sector
with the largest R and D expenditures for 1977. The survey excluded
R and D undertaken by Crown corporations, public utilities and private
firms in the areas of tar sands and atomic energy. The *Financial Post*
list of 35 R and D leaders is not all inclusive, but it is the only published
survey available and is worth some exploration. R and D is defined as
'all costs associated with the search for, and discovery of, new knowledge
that may be useful in developing new products, services, processes or
techniques, or that might significantly improve existing products or
processes'. Excluded are costs of routine product improvement or
seasonal changes of style, market research and testing, quality control
and legal costs to protect patents.

The 35 firms from this survey were divided initially into two groups:
independent Canadian firms and subsidiaries of multinational enterprises.
Data were then gathered from other sources on the sales, profits (defined
as net income after taxes) and, for the subsidiaries, percentage of
foreign ownership. Next the parent firms of the subsidiaries were
identified, to form a group of multinationals. The R and D, profits and
sales of the parents were then found, resulting in three groups of firms.

The samples are arranged in decreasing order of R and D expenditures
by the parent firms and by the independent Canadian firms. The subsidiaries are arranged according to the R and D of their parents, since
the theory of internalization predicts that the subsidiaries have no
independent R and D capability. An alternative method of arranging

the samples would have been to rank them by decreasing order of size, as proxied by sales. If this is done it can be observed that the ranking of the sample of independent Canadian firms is similar to that of the subsidiaries. Since the main focus of this research is upon R and D, ranking by this variable is the better method to use.

The limited availability of data on firm level R and D in Canada prevents sampling according to industry characteristics. Thus one of the weaker parts of this study is its neglect of the research intensity of some industry groups compared to others. Fortunately, some invest-igators of R and D have pitched their studies at industry level, for example Frankl (1979), Globerman (1973) and Hewitt (1980a). The present work complements these other studies but it cannot address itself to precisely the same questions as they do.

Due to data limitations several of the 35 firms had to be omitted. The basic source for the tables, 'Survey of 65 Corporations Concerning R and D Efforts Spotlighting 35 R and D Leaders in the Private Sector (1977)', *Financial Post* (10 June 1978), could not be reconciled fully with other data sources. Sales revenue and profit figures were obtained from the *Fortune 500* for parent firms, the *Financial Post 300* for most of the Canadian firms and the *Financial Post Survey of Industrials* for the remainder of the Canadian firms. R and D figures for the parent companies of the Canadian subsidiaries were obtained from a similar but more extensive survey undertaken by *Business Week* (3 July 1980). The following companies, from the survey, had to be omitted:

(a)   Alcan Aluminum – this company is neither a Canadian sub-sidiary nor is it a Canadian owned corporation since foreign ownership is 52.9 per cent in the United States and 13.6 per cent elsewhere.

(b)   Canadian International Paper – for this company, R and D figures for its parent company, International Paper, cannot be obtained.

(c)   Litton Systems – 1977 sales and profit figures cannot be obtained, and although 1976 and 1979 figures are available they introduce some potential error into the data.

(d)   Merck Frosst Laboratories – this company is owned 100 per cent by Merck and Co. Inc. of Raway, New Jersey. It is the manufacturing counterpart of Merck, Sharp and Dohme (IA) Corp. which manufactures pharmaceuticals for Merck, Sharp and Dohme Canada Ltd, and Charles E. Frosst & Co., both of whom are wholesalers. Strictly a manufacturing enterprise,

Merck Frosst Labs does not make available its sales and profit figures.

(e)   GTE Lenkurt – this company is a subsidiary of GTE Automatic Electric Canada Ltd (100 per cent ownership) which itself is owned (100 per cent) by General Telephone and Electronics. Data on sales and profits are not available for 1977. Data are available only for 1975 from the *Financial Post Information Service* and for 1979 from the *Canadian Key Business Directory 1980.* For GTE Lenkurt, sales in 1975 are $52 million, and in 1979 are $48.2 million.

(f)   AES Data Ltd – a Canadian company 100 per cent owned by the Canada Development Corp., i.e. by the Canadian Government. Data cannot be found for 1977. Sales figures are available for 1979 from the *Canadian Key Business Directory 1980*, and are $24.5 million.

(g)   Hawker-Siddeley Canada Ltd – a subsidiary of Hawker-Siddeley UK. Sales and profit figures are available but R and D expenditures cannot be obtained for the parent company.

(h)   CIL – a subsidiary of ICI of Britain, for which data are not available, except for another US affiliate.

(i)   Ayerst, McKenna and Harrison – a subsidiary of American Home Products. Data on sales and profits are not available for the appropriate year.

(j)   Leigh Instruments and Spar Aerospace. Data on sales and profits are not available for the appropriate year.

For the sample of Canadian subsidiaries the percentages of foreign ownership, obtained from the *Financial Post 300*, are:

Canadian General Electric and Marconi	75.1
Pratt & Whitney	100.0
duPont Canada	74.8
Xerox Canada	100.0
Imperial Oil	69.6
Dow Chemicals	100.0
Union Carbide	75.0
Westinghouse	93.3
NCR Canada	100.0
Shell Oil	71.0
Control Data	100.0
Gulf Oil Canada	68.3

It is apparent from Tables 6.3, 6.4 and 6.5 that the mean size of the parents is about ten times that of their subsidiaries. Yet mean R and D expenditures of the parents are 20 times those of their subsidiaries. The independent Canadian firms have mean sales that are 50 per cent greater than mean sales of subsidiaries. But their absolute mean expenditure on R and D is also 50 per cent greater than those of the subsidiaries. This implies that they do proportionately the same R and D as the subsidiaries, and much less than the parent multinationals, after allowing for size.

The ratios of R and D to sales present a more complicated picture. The mean ratio of R and D to sales for the sample of twelve parent firms is 3.12, well above the all industry composite for US manufacturing industry over the 1975-9 period, which averages 1.9. Consistent with the implications of internalization theory, the mean R and D to sales ratio for the twelve subsidiaries is 2.07, that is, lower than the ratio of the parent firms. In nine of the twelve actual firm cases the R and D to

Table 6.3: Expenditures on R and D by Twelve Multinational Firms in Canada, 1977 ($ Millions)

Parent firm	Sales ($US)	R and D ($US)	R and D sales (%)	Profits ($US)	R and D[a] profits (%)
General Electric	17,518	463.5	2.64	1,088.2	42.6
United Technology	5,551	368.3	6.63	195.9	188.0
duPont	9,435	366.8	3.89	545.1	67.3
Xerox	5,077	269.1	5.30	406.6	66.2
Exxon	54,126	230.0	0.43	2,422.9	9.5
Dow Chemicals	6,234	203.3	3.26	555.7	36.6
Union Carbide	7,036	155.8	2.21	385.1	40.5
Westinghouse	6,136	132.0	2.15	250.8	52.6
NCR	2,522	118.1	4.68	143.6	82.2
Shell Oil	10,112	91.0	0.90	735.1	12.4
Control Data	1,493	73.1	4.90	63.0	116.0
Gulf Oil	17,890	70.0	0.39	752.0	9.3
Mean			3.12		60.27

Note: a. R and D expenditures are not available for the Royal Dutch Shell group. The American affiliate is taken as an approximation.
Sources: Sales were obtained from 'Fortune 500', *Fortune* (May 1978). R and D expenditures were obtained from 'R and D Spending Patterns for 600 Companies', *Business Week* (3 July 1978).

sales ratio of the parent firm is greater than that of its subsidiary. The twelve independent Canadian firms have a mean ratio of R and D to sales of 1.19 which is lower than that of the subsidiaries and parents. In 1977 this sample of independent Canadian firms did less R and D than the parent multinationals themselves, and less than the subsidiaries.

Table 6.4: Expenditures on R and D by the Subsidiaries of Twelve Multinational Firms in Canada, 1977 ($ Millions)

Canadian subsidiary	Sales ($Cdn)	R and D ($Cdn)	R and D sales (%)	Profits ($Cdn)	R and D profits (%)
CGE & Cdn Marconi[a]	1,138.0	10.3	0.90	30.4	33.9
Pratt & Whitney	251.6	25.8	10.25	10.7	241.1
duPont Canada	534.5	5.3	0.99	7.6	69.7
Xerox Canada	294.6	3.9	1.32	27.0	14.4
Imperial Oil	4,970.0	20.7	0.42	289.0	7.2
Dow Chemicals	452.4	5.8	1.28	35.7	16.2
Union Carbide	406.5	1.4	0.34	20.5	6.8
Westinghouse	430.9	5.8	1.35	16.0	36.2
NCR	144.1	1.3	0.90	9.1	14.3
Shell Oil	2,349.3	12.0	0.51	154.6	7.8
Control Data	101.2	6.0	5.93	1.6	–
Gulf Oil	2,322.1	15.0	0.64	185.0	8.1
Mean			2.07		41.43

Note: a. Since Canadian General Electric (CGE) and Canadian Marconi are both subsidiaries of General Electric, the sum of their sales, and R and D are given. The Canadian Marconi data is for 1976 from '2 + 2', *Canadian Business* (July 1977). Sources: Sales were obtained from the 'Top 300 Industrial Comapnies', the *Financial Post* (Summer 1977). R and D expenditures were obtained from 'The Post Spotlights 35 R and D Leaders in the Private Sector', *Financial Post* (10 June 1978).

In a statistical analysis, in which the means for R and D to sales (for the samples of twelve firms) are tested for significant differences it is found that there are no significant differences between the respective means of the three samples, i.e. between 3.12, 2.07 and 1.19 on an F test (with an F ratio of 2.28), or between the subsidiaries and parents on a t test. Yet there is a significant difference between parent multinationals and independents on a t test. There is no significant difference between the mean of the R and D to sales ratio of the parent firms (3.12)

Table 6.5: Expenditures on R and D by Twelve Canadian Owned Corporations, 1977 ($ Millions)[a]

Canadian owned companies	Sales ($Cdn)	R and D ($Cdn)	R and D sales (%)	Profits ($Cdn)	R and D profit (%)
Bell Canada	3,559.9	112.9	3.17	268.2	39.45
Canada Development Corp.	708.8	24.0	3.38	23.8	100.84
Inco Metals	2,077.3	15.0	0.72	106.2	14.12
Steel Co. of Canada	1,444.0	6.8	0.47	90.2	7.54
MacMillan Bloedel	1,707.2	6.6	0.39	60.6	10.89
Massey Ferguson	2,935.9	5.2	0.18	34.2	15.20
CAE Industries	166.5	5.2	3.12	4.2	123.81
Canadian Pacific	4,700.0	4.9	0.10	239.8	2.04
Bombardier MLW	255.7	4.7	1.84	203.0	2.31
Domtar Inc.	1,009.5	4.5	0.44	26.8	16.79
Noranda Mines	1,386.5	4.5	0.32	67.2	6.70
Canada Packers	1,878.5	3.2	0.17	18.1	17.68
Mean			1.19		40.10

Note: a. Canadian owned companies are defined as those with foreign ownership less than 50 per cent.
Sources: Sales were obtained from the 'Top 300 Industrial Companies', *Financial Post* (Summer 1977). R and D expenditures were obtained from 'The Post Spotlights 35 R and D Leaders in the Private Sector', *Financial Post* (10 June 1978).

and that of the corresponding Canadian subsidiaries (2.07). The calculated t ratio, 1.01, for the data of these two groups, is less than the critical value of t for a two-tailed test at the 5 per cent confidence level. Similarly, the calculated t value for the means of the subsidiaries and independents is less than the required value. Yet there is a significant difference between the mean of the R and D to sales ratio of the parent firms (3.12) and of the independent Canadian owned firms (1.19). The calculated t ratio (2.77) for these two sets of firms is greater than the critical value for a two-tailed test at the 5 per cent confidence level.

Data on the ratio of R and D to profits rather than the ratio of R and D to profits are much the same as those presented above. The absolute and mean profits of the parent firms are almost ten times those of their subsidiaries, but the profits of independent Canadian firms are 50 per cent greater than those of foreign controlled subsidiaries. The mean ratio of R and D to profits varies by sample group, at 60.27 for parents, 41.43 for their subsidiaries and 29.78 for independent Canadian owned firms. The mean ratio of R and D to profits (given as percentages) show no significant difference between the mean ratio of parent firms (60.27) and that of their Canadian subsidiaries (41.43). Similarly, the mean ratios of R and D to profits for parent and Canadian owned firms, prove to be insignificantly different. In all three cases (parent-subsidiary, parent-Canadian and subsidiary-Canadian) the calculated t ratios, 0.739, 1.625 and 0.69 respectively, are less than the critical t statistic at the 5 per cent confidence level. The F ratio calculated (0.91) is less than the critical F value at the 5 per cent confidence level.

The ambiguous nature of some of these results is possibly due to the inadequate nature of the samples. These are constructed according to data availability and are probably not fully representative of the characteristics of the population of parent, subsidiary and independent Canadian firms. There is also a possibility that the firms included in the subsidiary and independent samples are not fully representative of the Canadian economy, or its technological variation across industries. When more firm level data on R and D become publicly available, further attempts at verification or refutation of the implications of internalization theory for R and D in Canada will become feasible. Until then, it is necessary to exercise suitable caution in the application of internalization theory to technology transfer in Canada and elsewhere.

Conclusions

In this chapter the theory of internalization has been utilized to explain the nature of the transfer of technology by multinational enterprises. While the results can be improved with some manipulation, such as the deletion of Pratt and Whitney which is a special case, I have chosen not to do so since there is sufficient support for my basic premise about the relative lack of R and D in subsidiaries. I believe that this methodology can be used to conduct more detailed tests when more firm level data on R and D become publicly available. Yet the basic application of internalization theory to technology transfer in Canada is the first step towards the formulation of a viable R and D policy which discriminates between foreign and domestic firms.

A major theme of this book is its demonstration of the misconceived nature of partial evaluations of the nation's welfare, such as the identification of outflows of payments for technology. These payments are not a problem *per se*, but are related directly to the pattern of protection in Canada, namely one of foreign ownership of its industry. The costs of technological payments by Canada have to be contrasted with the benefits of greater production and higher growth induced by multinational enterprises. In turn, the net costs of technology transfer must be identified with the Canadian economic policies which have encouraged foreign direct investment in the first place. A full analysis of technology transfer will thereby confront the inefficiencies of tariff policy and economic nationalism.

With the exceptions noted by the Science Council of Canada (1980) study of four successful world product mandates, there is abundant theoretical and empirical support for the observation that innovations and ongoing R and D expenditures are centralized in the home nation of the multinational enterprise. The diffusion of technology to host nations such as Canada takes place as a by-product of the strategic choice of the multinational enterprise, in which it generally prefers to retain control over its firm specific advantage in knowledge. Thus it uses the safer route of subsidiary production compared to the risky method of licensing, where there is a risk of dissipation of the firm specific advantage.

The preference of the typical multinational for internalization and control of its technology will make it very difficult for a host nation to alter the internal prices of the firm; indeed such attempts are likely to distort prices. The continuation of present Canadian science policies and non-discriminatory grants to both domestic and multinational firms is in conflict with the premises of internalization theory. It is necessary to consider more efficient alternatives. These include either direct subsidies for independent Canadian firms, that is discrimination against foreign owned firms, or the removal of market imperfections (such as tariffs) that have encouraged multinational activity in Canada in the first place.

7 THE REGULATION OF MULTINATIONAL CORPORATIONS

Introduction

Multinational enterprises are recognized as a dominant force in the world of today. European and Japanese based multinationals have rivalled US ones in their growth and economic impact on many nations in recent years. Undoubtedly multinationals are of great importance. Recently a new explanation of the multinational enterprise has been developed by economists, called the theory of internalization. In this section the implications of internalization theory are applied to answer questions concerned with the regulation of multinational enterprises by host nations such as Canada.

Canada is a wealthy nation; indeed it is one of the richest nations in the world. It is also a small, open economy, dominated by multinational corporations, mainly of US origin. Is Canada rich because of US foreign direct investment, or is it wealthy despite the pervasive presence of multinationals? This section addresses this issue—one which has caught the attention of generations of Canadian social scientists, but one which has never been fully reconciled.

As the principles of internalization theory are explained in the previous chapters, the present section assumes a knowledge of some economic theory and it sketches in an outline of internalization in a Canadian context. It then builds upon this foundation, and places primary emphasis upon the application of the new theory to the issue of regulation of multinationals in Canada. In this next section the principles of internalization theory are applied to the issue of regulation of multinationals in Canada. This extension of internalization theory in a Canadian context is required since the main contribution of the MNE to Canada is its ability to add net investment and technology to the economy. In fact, since the only advantages of the MNE are economic ones, these are identified here and explored at length. There are many other authors who choose to explore the political effects of the MNE and suggest that the MNE has sufficient economic power to bargain with the nation state. Yet we should be careful to catalogue the net economic benefits of the MNE in a precise manner, so that our natural concerns for sovereignty and independence do not lead us to confuse good economics with bad politics.

The second part of this chapter examines the performance of the 50 largest US based MNEs and contrasts this with the performance of the 50 largest non-American MNEs (mostly European or Japanese). Data on the profits of these firms over the last ten years are analyzed. If excessive profits are found it increases the strength of the argument for regulations of the MNEs. If profits are not excessive, the converse holds.

The final part of the chapter extends the issue of regulation of the MNE to less developed countries. It does so in terms of the equity versus efficiency trade-off implicit in economic theory in general and internalization theory in particular.

Regulation of the Multinational Enterprise in Canada

At least four arguments are advanced by those who favour increased regulation of the MNE. These are:

(a)   to preserve independence by the development of an indigenous manufacturing sector,

(b)   to improve sovereignty by the reduction of foreign ownership of major industrial or resource sectors,

(c)   to ensure an appropriate transfer of technology to the host nation,

(d)   to reduce the perceived excessive profits earned by MNEs.

Each of these arguments can be applied in a general manner to any host nation, either an advanced nation or a less developed economy. In this section these arguments are examined in the light of internalization theory, with special reference to Canada, although the general principles are widely applicable.

Internalization theory reveals that all of these arguments are excuses for protectionism. The industrialists of central Canada call for a tariff to raise the price of imported manufactured goods, such as textiles, in order to produce goods in excess of the world price but still sell to a captive domestic market. The original defence for tariffs was the infant industry argument, but this can hardly be valid in Canada some 100 years after Confederation.

The economic costs of tariffs are well known—see Eastman and Stykolt (1967) and Rugman (1980b). It is a strange type of national policy which calls for the persistent development of inefficient protected Canadian industry. Such high cost production is confined in a relatively small national market lacking scale economies for many industrial products. Furthermore, there are adverse regional effects for Canada, since the peripheral areas of west and Atlantic Canada must pay high prices for the inefficient manufactured goods of central Canada, yet still sell their resource based products at world prices. It would appear that Canada's independence is hindered by the perpetuation of regional inequalities stemming from its protectionist policy. Even to this day Canadian consumers continue to pay a heavy price for the support of inefficient central Canadian industry.

The other result of a protectionist policy is that the tariff acts as an inducement to foreign direct investment. Internalization theory implies that the multinational enterprise has been attracted to Canada by the tariffs here. Since the MNE could not fully service the Canadian market by the export mode it has been forced to go the subsidiary route. The result of 100 years of protection in Canada is the large amount of foreign ownership observed today. The best single method to reduce foreign ownership of the Canadian economy is to introduce free trade. Then foreign (mainly US) firms will choose to service the Canadian markets by exports.

Current attempts to make FIRA more restrictive to MNEs, or to 'negotiate' greater benefits for Canada are doomed to failure. The MNE may well engage in less subsidiary production, but it will simply circumvent FIRA by the use of more licensing agreements or by forming joint ventures. To re-emphasize the basic point, the existence of FIRA would be unnecessary in a world of free trade, as in such an unregulated world exporting would replace multinational activity.

The modern version of the protectionist creed is the infant technology argument. This calls for subsidies to firms (either foreign owned or independent Canadian) so that technology can be developed in new product lines. Then the firms are supposed to market the goods using the new technology, either through a world product mandate strategy, if they are foreign owned, or through exports proper if they are domestically owned. Only the latter case is likely to succeed, but the majority of subsidies for Canadian R and D still go to foreign owned, rather than independent, Canadian firms.

Internalization theory demonstrates that the appropriate technology for Canada is not one which results from a world product mandate strategy. Government subsidies which go to subsidiaries of foreign owned firms lead to a distortion of the internal prices of the MNEs involved. The theory of internalization predicts that R and D expenditures by subsidiaries do not result in genuine innovation but only adaptation of techniques at best. Instead, the subsidiaries exist primarily as extensions of the parent firm and their business is to safeguard the market of the MNE in the host nation. Through the use of its internal market the MNE monitors, controls and meters the use of its firm specific advantage in knowledge. The role of the subsidiary is supportive to the R and D function of the parent and it cannot be an innovator. Host nations, such as Canada, which attempt to reverse the forces of internalization do so at great risk and probably high cost.

The perceived need for regulation of the MNE is myopic. It has been demonstrated here and elsewhere that regulation of the MNE involves high economic costs. Canada's historical reliance on protection stems from an unfortunate choice which has placed greater emphasis upon the distributional goals of sovereignty and independence rather than upon the objective of economic efficiency. The result is the erection of unforeseen additional constraints on political independence in the form of foreign owned firms and poorer consumers, especially in the peripheral regions of Canada. The neglect of efficiency issues in the past has cost Canada dearly, and this should be a lesson for the future.

To summarize, there are at least four arguments given for regulation of the MNEs, but they are all questionable. The first is to preserve independent Canadian industry, yet we find that the MNE is attracted by the tariff (which was designed to protect Canadian industry). The second is to reduce American control of the economy, yet we observe that three-quarters of Canadian trade is with the USA anyway and the logic of geography dictates north-south trade. The third is to ensure an appropriate transfer of technology to Canada, yet the MNE is not an agent for development. This is the job of the government, and the optimal method for growth involves full utilization of foreign investment. The fourth is to reduce excessive profits of MNEs, yet studies reveal, see Vernon (1977) and Rugman (1979, 1980b), that they earn only 12 per cent return on equity, which is the same as the *Fortune* 1000, and is not indicative of rents or monopoly power being retained over time.

In conclusion, it is found that all arguments for regulation are false or misconceived. They stem from a concern for social, cultural or political objectives to the neglect of economic realities. All these arguments are based on faulty analyses or ignorance of the constraints placed upon Canadian trade and investment strategy. The MNE is an animal of the modern nation state. Internalization theory explains that it has developed to circumvent natural externalities and unnatural regulations. Further attempts at regulation will induce either more sophisticated MNEs or a shift towards joint ventures and licensing. Either of the latter two outcomes will increase welfare costs for Canada and generate new inefficiencies.

Conclusions on Regulation of the MNE

In this section the theory of internalization has been applied in a Canadian context and has examined the issue of regulation of multinationals. The internal market of the MNE is a mechanism by which it monitors the use of its firm specific advantage in knowledge. Internalization is a superior device to licensing or joint ventures from the viewpoint of the MNE, as the risk of dissipation of its firm specific advantage is minimized. Clearly the MNE is not in business to transfer technology to Canada or to otherwise intervene in its affairs but it is here to make profits over time, a market test which requires the cautious use of resources and technology by the firm. The lack of technological independence in Canada is not the fault of the MNE but is determined by Canadian industrial policy. Multinationals tend to respond to market imperfections, such as tariffs, rather than to promote them. An increased role for FIRA will either deter the MNE, at high costs to the Canadian consumer, or it will lead to more licensing and joint venture agreements when these are not the optimal modes of servicing the Canadian market.

Nationalists have argued that tariffs and subsidies are necessary to protect Canadian industry. Instead, foreign direct investment has resulted. Internalization theory shows that the subsidiaries of the multinational enterprises are usually miniature replicas of the parents. Consequently, there is relatively little R and D done in the subsidiaries. Nor is this a problem for Canada, since the nation enjoys benefits of greater production, employment and wealth resulting from multinational activity.

The future for industry in Canada will be improved more by removal of tariffs, and other restrictions and guidelines facing foreign direct investment, than by policies to promote domestic R and D. The current panacea of a world product mandate is misconceived since internalization theory demonstrates that the subsidiaries of multinational firms are in import competing sectors. Consequently, subsidiaries are unlikely to be very successful in the export of technology. In the long run a different (but efficient) type of independent Canadian industry can emerge which will be able to compete internationally. This will occur only when tariffs, foreign investment regulations, FIRA and artificial subsidies are removed so that the principles of free trade can operate. In the meantime Canadian science policy, which involves giving subsidies to foreign owned firms, is an inefficient use of public funds. It results from a misconception of the role of multinational enterprises in Canada.

Multinationals are here in the first place because of tariffs and other types of protective devices. Further regulation of multinational enterprises in Canada is not called for. Instead, public policy should seek to reduce the market imperfections which have enticed the multinationals to Canada. The multinational enterprise is an institutional response to regulations and lack of regular markets. Internalization theory explains why it exists and how it operates. The multinational is not a strange animal, but rather a robust and efficient organization operating in an imperfect world.

Performance of Multinational Enterprises

Evidence on the performance of the MNE is available and it should give us information about the necessity for either more or less regulation of the MNE in the future. If we observe excessive profits being earned by MNEs it presents a solid argument for regulation. Yet if excessive profits are not found then the case for regulation is weakened.

Table 7.1 reports data on the profits of the 50 largest US based multinational enterprises. To be included in the table the MNE is defined as having a ratio of foreign to total operations (F/T) of 30 per cent or more. Sales (F/T) are used, and when these sales data are not available, or are ambiguous, data on assets are used (for a total of six cases only). Data on (F/T) are available from Bruck and Lees (1968) and from the United Nations source cited in the notes to Table 7.1.

There is some potential for misuse of the (F/T) ratio as an index of multinationality since it includes exports from the home nation as well as production by overseas affiliates. Unfortunately, for most of these firms, there is no way of separating out these two types of international activity, so the listing should be interpreted with this caveat in mind. The choice of a 30 per cent (F/T) is also somewhat arbitrary and firms with a lower (F/T) could have been included, for example General Motors has an (F/T) of 24 per cent, so it failed to make the cut. If a broader group of firms were to be included – say those with an (F/T) of over 20 per cent – it is unlikely that any difference would occur in the results.

Table 7.1: Performance of the Largest US Multinationals, 1970-9

Rank	Name	Index of multinationality	Mean profits	Risk of profits
1	Exxon	72	14.90	2.96
3	Mobil	49*	13.22	2.71
4	Ford Motor	31	12.21	4.57
5	Texaco	54	12.74	3.19
6	Standard Oil of California	59	13.06	2.78
7	Gulf Oil	55	11.36	3.64
8	International Business Machines	50	18.73	2.22
10	Standard Oil (Ind.)	34*	13.68	3.37
11	International Tel. and Tel.	49	11.05	2.00
13	Shell Oil	62	12.63	3.24
15	Conoco (formerly Continental Oil)	41	13.96	4.08
17	Chrysler	28	4.26	5.33
21	Occidental Petroleum	47	13.44	12.06
22	Phillips Petroleum	49*	13.85	5.04
24	Dow Chemical	46	18.41	5.64
25	Union Carbide	62	12.71	3.68
26	United Technologies	41	11.63[a]	1.87
27	International Harvester	37	8.92	3.96
28	Goodyear Tire & Rubber	38	9.68	1.89
29	Boeing	48	10.55	8.25
30	Eastman Kodak	39	17.94	1.79
33	Caterpillar Tractor	58	17.63	2.99
34	Union Oil of California	30	11.80	3.40
37	Westinghouse Electric	31	8.65[b]	2.87
40	Xerox	44	18.04	2.48
48	Monsanto	30	12.40	4.14
51	Minnesota Mining and Manufacturing	39	18.34	2.32
53	Firestone Tire & Rubber	34	8.15	3.43
55	W.R. Grace	30	11.00	3.67
59	Coca-Cola	44	21.47	1.32
60	Deere	31	14.25	3.70
61	Colgate Palmolive	55	13.99	2.20
63	Aluminum Co. of America	31*	9.62	4.82
66	International Paper	30	12.22	5.33
68	TRW	35	14.73	1.84
71	Weyerhaeuser	31	15.42	4.53
72	Continental Group	33	10.78	4.26

Rank	Name	Index of multinationality	Mean profits	Risk of profits
78	Johnson & Johnson	41	16.57	0.71
79	Honeywell	32	10.86	2.62
80	Sperry (formerly Sperry Rand)	43	11.27	1.81
81	Litton Industries	33*	5.49	6.03
89	American Brands	49	13.87	3.01
93	CPC International	55	15.70	2.17
97	United Brands	69*	2.19	1.79
98	Dresser Industries	38	13.91	3.62
99	American Home Products	31	28.02	1.43
100	Textron	34	14.46	1.08
105	Warner-Lambert	45	14.19	1.98
111	NCR	49	10.25	7.37
134	Uniroyal	36	4.90	2.96
Average for all 50 companies			12.98	4.38

Notes: a. 1971 data unavailable. b. 1979 data unavailable.
   Ranking by sales for 1979 is from the *Fortune 500*. Profits are defined as net income after taxes divided by the value of the stockholders' equity.
   Risk of profits is shown by standard deviation over 1970-9.
   Index of Multinationality is represented by the ratio of foreign to total sales for 1976 and when this is not available by the ratio of foreign to total assets, shown by a * for 1976. From Table IV-1 of United Nations Economic and Social Council, *Transnational Corporations in World Development: A Re-Examination* (1978).

The profits of the MNEs are defined as return on equity, i.e. net income after taxes divided by the value of shareholders' equity. These data are readily available from annual issues of the *Fortune 500*. Mean and standard deviation of profits were calculated for each firm for a ten year span from 1970 to 1979. Based on a mean variance model of portfolio theory, mean profits represent the expected rate of return and the standard deviation is a proxy for risk of earnings.

The average profit for all 50 MNEs is 12.98 per cent, while the risk of profits (proxied by the standard deviation) is 4.38 per cent. As the mean profit rate for all the firms in the *Fortune 500* is between 12 and 13 per cent over this decade it is clear that the large MNEs are not generating earnings which are significantly different from US industry in general. Only two of the 50 MNEs earned over 20 per cent return on equity in this period, and only a total of six had a return on equity of 18 per cent or greater, i.e. earned 50 per cent more than the mean profit rate for all firms of about 12 per cent. Offsetting these firms with excessive profits are a group of MNEs with very low returns. Indeed the distribution of returns is approximately symmetrical.

The finding that most MNEs earn a normal rate of return has an important implication. It is that, as a group, MNEs are efficient. With very few exceptions (only six out of the largest 50 US based MNEs) individual MNEs are also efficient. They are unable to export their firm specific advantage (a monopoly position) to generate excess profits over time. Indeed, most of the MNEs do only as well as the all industry average.

The all industry average can be proxied by taking the mean return on equity over 1970-9 for all the firms in the *Fortune 500*, giving a figure of 12.85 per cent. The means for individual years (shown in parentheses) are: 1970 (10.29); 1971 (10.06); 1972 (11.04); 1973 (12.81); 1974 (13.81); 1975 (12.34); 1976 (13.49); 1977 (13.90); 1978 (14.27); 1979 (16.47). The increase in mean return on equity in the last few years is of interest. The standard deviation of the ten years means is 1.98 per cent. The same picture emerges if median return on equity is used, instead of the mean. The median return on equity for the *Fortune 500*, over the 1970-9 period, is 12.35 per cent, with a standard deviation of 2.20.

There are seven of the 50 largest US based multinationals earning excessive profits over the 1970-9 period, where excess profits are defined as those approximately 50 per cent or more above the all industry mean return on equity for the *Fortune 500* of 12.85 per cent for the ten years. These firms (with their return on equity figures in parentheses) are: IBM (18.73); Dow Chemical (18.41); Eastman Kodak (17.94); Xerox (18.04); Minnesota Mining and Manufacturing (18.34); Coca-Cola (21.47); American Home Products (28.02). Over the 1968-77 period the profits of Eastman Kodak were 18.23 per cent, so this firm has been included in the list, although its profits were slightly under 18 per cent for the seventies.

As an offset of these seven very profitable US multinationals there are four US based multinationals out of the largest 50 group that have extremely poor earnings, where these are defined as profits 50 per cent or more below the all industry average return on equity of 12.85 per cent over the 1970-9 period. These US multinationals with poor earnings (with their return on equity shown in parentheses) are: Chrysler (4.26); Litton (5.49); United Brands (2.19) and Uniroyal (4.90). The results of the poor performance of Chrysler (ranked in 1979 as the seventeenth largest firm in the US) are well known and, if its economic and financial troubles are representative, then other members of this group of poor performers may well face similar problems in the near future. It is note-worthy that the remaining 40 multinationals out of the group of 50 do not have either excessive profits or excessively poor earnings as these terms are defined here.

Given the normal distribution of profits for the US multinationals it would seem reasonable to conclude that their further regulation is un-warranted. The data refute claims that these giant US multinationals are exploiting foreign nations. Instead they are only doing as well as the rest of US business; the very profitable multinationals being offset by poor performers. Indeed these results imply that the present state of imperfect international markets acts as a sufficient barrier to US multinationals. On the average we observe that their firm specific advantages and internal markets are only able to generate normal profits.

Table 7.2 examines the performance of the 50 largest non-US based multinationals. The methodology of Table 7.1 is repeated, i.e. mean and standard deviation of profits are calculated over the 1970-9 period for firms with a (F/T) ratio of 30 per cent or greater.

As a group these non-US multinationals earn only 9.54 per cent on equity, which is considerably less than that of the US multinationals. Indeed, the performance of the non-US firms is even worse than is indicated by the mean return since six of the firms reported losses for at least one of the ten years. All such negative returns are taken as zero in the calculations of mean and standard deviation, thus tending to bias upwards the results, to a small degree. The risk of profits is similar for both groups of MNEs.

One reason for the patchy performance of these non-US multi-nationals is the influence of the public sector on several of the firms, which are really state owned enterprises rather than private sector multinationals. The reasons for state ownership of several of the non-US firms need not be gone into here, but it is noticeable that their perform-ance is relatively poorer than that of US private sector multinationals. The influence of state owned enterprises in Europe, and the reasons for their growth are discussed in Mazzolini (1979) while the spread of these public corporations and their competitive threat to traditional multinationals is described in Walters and Monsen (1979).

There are only four non-US multinationals with excessive profits, where these are defined as rate of return on equity of approximately 50 per cent above the average return of about 10 per cent for the group as a whole. These firms (with their rates of return in parentheses for the 1970-9 period) are: Royal Dutch Shell (16.24); Toyota (16.2); the

Table 7.2: Performance of the Largest Non-US Multinationals 1970-9

Rank	Name	Country	Index of multinationality	Mean profits	Risk of profits
1	Royal Dutch/Shell	Netherlands/UK	62	16.24	6.37
2	British Petroleum	UK	83	12.10	7.81
3	Unilever	UK/Netherlands	48	13.64	3.65
6	Francaise des Pétroles	France	54	11.72	12.22
7	Peugeot-Citroën	France	47	11.12	7.48
8	Volkswagenwerk	Germany	62	8.05[b]	7.21
9	Phillips	Netherlands	37	6.49	2.21
10	Renault	France	45	2.15[b1]	3.59
11	Siemens	Germany	50	8.99	1.53
12	Daimler-Benz	Germany	60	14.65	3.68
13	Hoechst	Germany	67	8.07	3.07
14	Bayer	Germany	75	9.07	1.90
15	BASF	Germany	45	8.84	2.15
17	Toyota Motor	Japan	35	16.20	3.93
20	Nestlé	Switzerland	97	10.25	.88
21	Nissan Motor	Japan	66	13.01	3.50
23	Nippon Steel	Japan	32	7.61	3.93
24	Mitsubishi Heavy Industries	Japan	34	8.35	3.65
25	Imperial Chemical Industries	UK	61	12.81	3.21
26	Matsushita Electrical Industrial	Japan	31	12.24	4.43
28	BAT Industries	UK	88	13.32	1.34
30	Saint-Gobain-Pont-a-Mousson	France	58	6.95	2.48
32	Generale d'Electricité	France	37	6.00	2.24
33	Montedison	Italy	41	3.23[f]	7.10
35	Pechiney Ugine Kuhimann	France	47	5.81[a]	3.65
36	Rhone-Poulene	France	57	4.97[b]	3.43
38	Petrofina	Belgium	95*	13.04	2.07
40	Thomson Brandt	France	36	14.30	12.27
41	Fried Krupp	Germany	38	6.20[a2]	5.41
44	Mannesmann	Germany	70	12.35	7.63
46	AEG Telefunken	Germany	44	4.35[e]	7.72
47	ESTEL	Netherlands/Germany	37	4.72[d]	5.58
51	DSM	Netherlands	68	10.56	9.07

Rank	Name	Country	Index of multinationality	Mean profits	Risk of profits
52	British Leyland	UK	54	4.94[c]	4.44
53	Michelin	France	61	10.10	2.58
55	Akzo Group	Netherlands	88	5.56[c]	4.75
57	Nippon Kokan	Japan	34	7.53	4.52
59	Ciba-Geigy	Switzerland	98	2.67	1.20
60	Robert Bosch	Germany	51	11.24	2.94
63	Gutehoffnungshutte	Germany	45	6.87	2.13
65	Volvo	Sweden	68	11.61	6.52
66	Sumitomo Metal Industries	Japan	47	7.13[3]	3.35
67	Rio Tinto-Zinc	UK	81	10.84	3.40
73	General Electric	UK	50	15.85	5.49
74	Kawasaki Steel	Japan	37	8.25	4.82
78	Kobe Steel	Japan	37	6.55	3.04
79	Alcan Aluminum	Canada	84	26.02	50.64
82	Guest, Keen & Nettlefolds	UK	42	6.53	2.36
125	Massey Ferguson	Canada	92	7.69[b]	5.92
156	Tate & Lyle	UK	42	10.24[4]	5.40
Average for all 50 companies				9.54	4.31

Notes: a. negative returns for 1 year. b. negative returns for 2 years. c. negative returns for 3 years. d. negative returns for 4 years. e. negative returns for 5 years. f. negative returns for 6 years. 1. 1976 data not available. 2. 1979, 1978, 1977 data not available. 3. 1973 data not available. 4. 1975 data not available.

Ranking is by sales for 1979 from the *Fortune 500* list of the Largest Non-US Firms.

Profits are defined as net incomes after taxes divided by the value of stockholders' equity. Risk of profits is shown by the standard deviation on 1970-9.

Index of multinationality is from the same source as Table 7.1.

UK General Electric (15.85) and Alcan of Canada (26.02). Other firms running close behind are Daimler-Benz (14.65) and Thomson Brandt (14.3).

In contrast to these very profitable MNEs there is a group of very unsuccessful MNEs, six of which made losses in at least one year. The eight non-US MNEs with poor earnings, i.e. under 5 per cent return on equity are: Renault (2.15); Montedison (3.23); Rhone-Poulenc (4.97); AEG Telefonken (4.35); Estel (4.72); Leyland (1.94); Ciba-Geigy (2.67); and a firm, Akzo, for which the mean rate of return of 5.56 per cent is biased upwards since it excludes three years of negative returns.

The finding that some 20 per cent of the 50 largest non-US multi-nationals are doing very badly in terms of poor earnings is a warning to those seeking to impose further controls on the MNEs. Several of these firms are on the verge of collapse, such as British Leyland, Massey-Ferguson and Renault. These MNEs may have neglected to retain their firm specific advantages, or found the costs of the internal market to exceed the benefits, or even been rendered uncompetitive by excessive labour or government manipulation of their organizational structure. Their poor performance demonstrates that internalization has its limits.

Multinationals in Developing Nations

In the remainder of the chapter I turn from a consideration of the implications of internalization theory in a Canadian context to a wider analysis of the relevance of this theory for less developed countries. The field of development economics has generated many terms for these countries. Historically the terminology has changed from 'underdeveloped nations' to 'less developed countries', and has included developing nations, poorer nations and terms such as 'Third World' or 'the South'. I shall use this terminology interchangeably to refer to those nations in the southern hemisphere with low *per capita* real incomes.

Biersteker (1978) compares and evaluates two contending paradigms of the effects of multinational enterprises (MNEs) on development. These alternative theoretical perspectives are identified as first, the 'critical perspective' of dependency theory and, secondly, the 'neoconventional perspective' of economists such as Ray Vernon and his colleagues, who have participated in the Harvard Business School's MNE project. Biersteker gives a thorough taxonomic account of these perspectives, in Chapters 1 and 2 respectively, and then points up their major areas of agreement and disagreement in Chapter 2. Here he makes a useful distinction between matched arguments, where contending propositions can be contrasted, and mismatched arguments, 'in which the two approaches direct their arguments past each other' (p. 49). In the remaining half of the book the author applies his theoretical analysis to a case study of multinational investment in Nigeria.

The findings of the theoretical section are neatly summarized in a series of seven tables. In each of the first two chapters are listed the main points made by proponents of each perspective, with, in Chapter 3, the author's interpretation of matched and mismatched arguments about the impact of the MNE on development. The seven topics are:

balance of payments effects; displacement of indigenous production; extent of technology transfer; appropriateness of the technology; patterns of consumption; local social structures; and income distribution effects. Given the emotional nature of much of the criticism of the MNE, the author is to be congratulated on his excellent analytical statement of the critical perspective and his balanced assessment of it and the contending neoconventional perspective. On methodological grounds some economists might quibble with this approach, since not all the contending propositions can be tested. Yet it is a useful contribution to have the nonaddressed arguments and mismatched propositions of the two paradigms expressed explicitly. It may help the two camps understand each other's work, instead of persisting in the common practice of ignoring it.

The empirical work of Chapters 4 to 8 is based on an interesting case study of Nigeria which uses an elaborate data base (described in an appendix) with information on 60 economic and financial variables for a sample of foreign and domestic firms in the industry groups of textiles, cement, sawmilling and sugar refining. Data for the 1963-72 period are collected for 60 firms, giving a total of 293 cases after allowing for missing or unreliable data. There may be more of the latter than the author believes since some of the financial information on capital sourcing, remitted profits, dividends and transfer pricing came from interviews with firm accountants and managers.

The information from such interviews will probably incorporate many subjective biases and is less reliable than the data from the Central Bank and Industrial Survey Division of the Government Statistics Office. Fortunately most data come from these official sources.

Biersteker does not find much evidence from his field work on Nigeria to support the critical perspective of the MNE. For example, in Chapter 5 he reports that local financing predominates (as it does elsewhere), exporting is substantial, transfer pricing does not exist and the remission of profits is not a problem. Although there is a net outflow of capital from MNEs in manufacturing, this outflow is trivial relative to Nigeria's oil revenues. Due to the abundant foreign exchange reserves there has been less tension in Nigeria between the MNE and nation-state than in other developing nations. Indeed, dependency theory seems less applicable to Africa, in general, than to Latin America.

I have two comments on this chapter. First, when testing the linkages hypothesis (p. 90) I think that the imports percentage should be treated as an independent variable rather than as a dependent variable, since in the present form only a couple of dummy variables are significant and size is not — a surprising result. Secondly, the author argues that when Biafra was blockaded during the civil war the region was able to develop indigenous production, even in the relatively sophisticated technology of petroleum refining. He says that 'the Biafran case suggests that feasible alternatives to the multinational corporation exist in Nigeria' (p. 100). Yet this historical situation seems more an example of response to war conditions than a scientific experiment in alternative technology. Further, the author ignores the basic question of costs and fails to ask if such indigenous production is efficient. But perhaps such comments are too 'neoconventional'?

In a major essay Carlos Diaz-Alejandro (1978) writes on delinking North and South. His criticisms of *laissez faire* as a false strategy in a world full of market imperfections and second-best solutions are well made. Perhaps surprising to some of his readers will be his rejection of the polar opposite case, namely pure delinking. He believes that such a policy of national self sufficiency is as impossible in today's interdependent world as is the *laissez faire* policy of development by free trade. In practice we have both economic linkages between nations and political constraints (in the form of regulations, tariffs and taxes) on a pure market solution to development problems. Thus Diaz-Alejandro steers a middle course in recommending selective delinking for the South. This policy will bring in some of the benefits of Northern technology and production skills while allowing the South to avoid some of the costs of the existing world economic order, such as commodity price fluctuations, deteriorating terms of trade and other foreign exchange problems. However, he does not support a Prebisch-type policy of self reliant industrialization to replace trade, even for large nations, since the South cannot escape completely the worldwide influence of Northern capital and technology.

The rejection of Diaz-Alejandro of the strong form of the delinking hypothesis leads to the same general conclusions as those reached by Albert Fishlow (1978) in a more conventional economic theory approach. Fishlow argues that the world economic order can be reformed satisfactorily by removal of tariff barriers and by increased financial flows (in the form of private direct investment) to less developed countries (LDCs). Therefore both economists end up advocating development within the framework of a reformed international economy rather than by turning to self reliant industrialization. These conclusions differ sharply from those of political scientists such as Wriggens and Adler-Karlsson (1978). The latter writers do not appear to understand the efficiency considerations of concern to economists. Instead they focus upon socioeconomic and political arguments that decry the dependency of LDCs on the North. Thus they tend to advocate more radical changes in the world economic order, such as that of Adler-Karlsson for self reliant political decentralization to the village level. It is to be hoped that the laudable concern with world equity does not destroy the world economy by adoption of inefficient policies of self reliance, policies which are especially inappropriate for the smaller LDCs.

The underlying assumption in the essays by these authors is that the South has not been receiving an equitable share of the world's wealth and power. Several of the authors use this assumption to argue for policies that will either reform the present system or radically change it. In doing so they examine the perceived inefficiencies of the world system which have led to the inequitable distribution of income between North and South. Yet, as any well trained economist knows, equity and efficiency are different animals and they cannot be easily reconciled. Therefore it is worth making a very simple point, namely that if an inequitable world income distribution is being assumed, the correct method to change it is by a worldwide system of taxes and subsidies. Ultimately world income can only be redistributed through taxation of the richer nations and subsidies to the poorer ones. Since such redistribution policies are ineffective within nation-states, even when they have strong governments, we should not be surprised at the failure of such policies on an international level where there exists no strong central authority. The unhappy conclusion is that the achievement of an equitable distribution of the world's wealth requires a genuine policy of international redistribution of income, but such a policy is likely to be, in practice, an impossible dream.

A common theme by non-economists such as Solomon (1978) is the familiar one that the MNEs possess excessive political and economic power and need to be regulated in order to foster the growth of poorer nations. These writers (Solomon being a lawyer) swallow the dependency theory uncritically and, amongst other errors, suggest that the MNEs are inimical to well rounded development and that they generate excess profits. With reference to the first point it is clear to me that the MNE is not a development agency and that the government of the host nation bears responsibility for development and income distribution, and through taxation and other economic policies it can achieve these goals. Secondly, there is a growing body of empirical work which demonstrates that MNEs earn profits which are not significantly different from non-MNEs and finds no evidence of transfer pricing, at least as reflected in the performance of MNEs. Nor is it clear that the Eurodollar market needs to be regulated, as Solomon claims in Chapter 4, since it developed largely through regulation of the domestic US banking system. All in all the new transnational social order is a much trickier subject than these writers seem to understand.

Hymer (1979) a self-proclaimed Marxist, attempted to advance a radical critique of the MNE. These papers stand in sharp contrast to his 1960 doctoral dissertation, when, still a liberal economist, he developed a brilliant original analysis of the MNE based upon the market imperfect-ions approach. While his dissertation has been very influential in subsequent work on the theory of the MNE it is not clear that his radical papers do anything more than preach to the converted. The papers anticipate many of our current policy problems as nation states, especially in developing countries, attempt to confront the perceived economic power of the MNE. Such perceptions are reinforced by Hymer's emphasis upon the internationalization of capital and his argument that the MNE hinders economic development. Yet those of us who are more concerned with efficiency than the Marxist emphasis upon distribution alone cannot accept much of Hymer's radical analysis. Regulation of the MNE is somewhat myopic, since it involves foregone economic opportunities. Although Hymer has raised relevant questions of political economy which need to be debated by all students of the MNE, his later work does not provide any panaceas for regulation of the MNE.

Bergsten, Horst and Moran (1978) in an ambitious book undertake the difficult task of integrating the economic and political aspects of American multinational activities as they affect US public policy. They examine the contribution of multinationals to the home economy in chapters on the balance of payments, labour, resources, taxation, com-petition and anti-trust policy, trade and exports and the international monetary system. Political issues of multinationals are discussed in the context of American foreign policy towards developing and industrial-ized countries. Their approach is to summarize the major theoretical and empirical contributions to the recent literature on multinationals, a task which is achieved in a reasonably balanced manner, and to report some new empirical work on the profitability and other economic characteristics of US multinationals.

One of their key findings is that US tax policy towards multinationals is close to neutrality and that 'as a general rule multinationals do not escape taxation by investing overseas'. Another is that exports and foreign direct investment seem to be complementary. Yet another is that there is little statistical support for the notion 'that the surge in foreign direct investment over the last decades significantly affected income shares' to the detriment of labour. More surprising are the results on page 241 which show that the earnings (on assets) for groups of US multinationals are greater than for groups of domestic firms. In some of the work reported in this book I find that earnings (on equity) are about the same for multinational and uninational firms. Here the authors use their new (industrial-level) data on the profitability of multinationals to conclude that the oligopolistic structure of these firms needs to be modified. They advocate increased anti-trust activity and even the divestment of some foreign subsidiaries to reduce the market power of US multinationals. This work on profitability is somewhat controversial and it should be interpreted with caution.

It will be interesting to see if the 'Brookings view' of the world leads to greater US regulation of multinationals. If so, we may expect to witness the demise of many American multinationals since they will then be subject to major economic controls in their home nation in addition to the severe barriers being erected by the governments of many host nations. The concern for equity, manifest in their book, may well compromise the efficiency of multinational firms.

Multinationals from Small Countries[1]

If there is a theory of economic development, it is subject to constant change. Indeed the field is probably too large to produce a satisfactory theory which can integrate all of the areas studied by development economists (and non-economists). Development economists need to focus on the role and activity of a principal agent in developing nations — the multinational enterprise (MNE). The fashionable nature of work on the MNE in the recent literature needs to be incorporated into the theory of development.

Agmon and Kindleberger (1977) have done so in a recent book in which they identified a gap in the literature on the MNE. They invited seven authors to write papers dealing with the foreign investment undertaken by MNEs based in 'small' nations. Many of us are used to thinking of the MNEs as originating in the United States, Western Europe, or, perhaps, Japan. This book does not study such MNEs. Instead, the writers consider MNEs based in the 'small' nations of Latin America, France, Sweden, Switzerland and Australia. Canada is, unfortunately, not examined although it has proportionately more inward and outward foreign direct investment (FDI) than any other country and, in the terminology of the book, is a small nation *par excellence.*

The papers of greatest interest to development economists are those by Carlos Diaz-Alejandro of Yale and Louis Wells of the Harvard Business School. These authors deal with FDI in Latin America and 'developing countries' respectively. The main points of these papers are discussed below. The book also features papers by Niehans on Switzerland, Carlson on Sweden, Bertin on France and Hughes on technology transfer in Australia. These papers are of uneven quality· and are not always directed towards the central issue of small country MNEs.

Rather than give a summary of each paper, I shall, instead, concentrate on three central themes which emerge from the book. These are: first, the extent to which a common theory of foreign direct investment (FDI) is recognized by the authors of the more theoretical papers; secondly, the argument raised by several writers that small scale MNEs are efficient in small nations and can assist in the development process; thirdly, the roles of the public sector and political factors in an analysis of the MNE.

The modern theory of FDI is recognized explicitly by the majority of the authors. This theory is attributed to the seminal work by Hymer (1976) in which he hypothesized that the MNE would exploit abroad an advantage acquired in one or more of the many segments of the product and factor markets. The ability of the MNE to create an internal market to substitute for the missing external market for knowledge, information, research and technological skills has been recognized in more recent work by Buckley and Casson (1976). The latter refinement of Hymer's market imperfections hypothesis is not developed by the economists writing in the volume, nor does an explicit statement of it appear anywhere. This is unfortunate since the concept of internalization advanced by Buckley and Casson is a potential unifying theory of FDI, and until it becomes accepted as a general theory much of the writing on the MNE will continue to be unstructured.

The most stimulating and provocative paper in the book is that by Agmon and Lessard. In their essay they concentrate on the capital market imperfections faced by the MNEs operating abroad. They list as many as 13 imperfections in financial markets that can affect MNEs based in small nations. These include: foreign exchange controls; different national tax rates; restrictions on foreign investment; information and transactions costs; constraints on the domain of contracts; government regulations affecting interest rates, credit allocations and securities; and the small size or thinness of many overseas financial markets. The authors argue that 'some of these effects can be offset by the existence of conglomerate business groups that internalize many capital market functions'. As far as I can recall this is the only explicit mention of internalization in the whole book, but even here the authors do not take up the point and instead choose to emphasize the related concept of international diversification.

In a world of capital market imperfections, it is impossible for an individual investor, especially one based in a small nation, to purchase shares in the corporations of various nations. Therefore the benefits of risk reduction through international diversification can only be achieved in an indirect manner—by the purchase of shares in an MNE which has a stable stream of earnings over time due to its production and sales in nations where factor and goods markets are not perfectly correlated with those of the investor, see Rugman (1979).

Agmon and Lessard accept the point that the MNE is a surrogate vehicle for international diversification only in passing and do not make enough of it. In my opinion it is of central importance to their study, yet their thinking is apparently still dominated by vestiges of capital market theory which are relevant only in a world of integrated capital markets (as they would readily agree). Thus, that paper is not as precise as it could be and does not develop its very stimulating arguments with sufficient clarity or in enough detail. Despite this I suggest that it be read first by those with a more theoretical inclination, since it sets the stage for the excellent essay by Jurg Niehans.

Niehans probably has one of the best analytical minds in the profession, and his incursion into the realm of political economy in this paper on small MNEs in Switzerland is full of good theoretical insights. He examines the intermediate product flows to these MNEs and works in both the market imperfections and international diversification aspects of the theory of FDI to explain the flows. Next he twists the theory of FDI to help explain the key characteristic of the MNE, as he sees it, which is the scale advantage resulting from the vertical integration of production. His major hypothesis is derived from two counterfactual exercises in which the contribution of five large MNEs to the Swiss economy is evaluated by assuming them away and examining the economy in their absence. In the first exercise protection is assumed away which leads, naturally, to more foreign trade and welfare gains. There is a relative contraction of MNEs—due to the fact that the incentive for their formation (in the form of a tariff) has been removed. In the second exercise other types of market imperfections (which lead to the emergence of the MNE) are assumed away, with a smaller gain in efficiency, since technology transfer is reduced.

Niehans concludes that the MNE is a second-best method for small nations, such as Switzerland, to achieve vital economies of scale. In a perfect world with no barriers to trade the MNE is unnecessary. However, in the real world characterized by government imposed regulations, tariffs, and other market imperfections it is an agency which 'helps to equalize the economic opportunities between firms of small and large countries'. The comment by Michael Adler on this paper raises some further theoretical issues which cannot be discussed here, although they are of interest. Instead, I now take up the point about scale since this is the second major theme identified.

Two authors argue that MNEs in small nations can be efficient at adapting technology to the requirements of the nations. Helen Hughes uses Australia as a case study of transfer of technology both to a small nation (itself) and also from it to developing nations in South-east Asia and its neighbour Papua New Guinea. She thinks that, in general, it is necessary to 'scale down' technology for the Australian market. Once MNEs have done this they can then act as technological intermediaries in the servicing of markets in developing nations. In practice there is insufficient latitude given to the subsidiaries of major MNEs by their parent firms, with the result that there is a lack of adaptation of technology to the needs of low income nations. Hughes believes that Australia could be a much better intermediary in the transfer of technology than it has been so far. She is also a good enough economist to place part of the blame on the inward looking policies of Australian governments. Protection has encouraged inward FDI but it has not fostered outward FDI.

I do not find this as surprising as Hughes does, since the tariff will encourage an inefficient manufacturing sector to develop. A protected industry is unlikely to be characterized by innovation, research or adaptation of technology. Instead, as shown by Sune Carlson in his essay on the internationalization process, a nation (such as Sweden) which is committed more to free trade than to protection will be more successful in both the absorption and re-export of technology. To an extent, Carlson's thesis is derived from consideration of marketing factors rather than purely production ones. Yet he does demonstrate that an outward looking small nation can have successful MNEs of its own.

The second writer to advocate the adaptation of technology as the major role for MNEs from small nations is Louis Wells. He believes in this as a possible model for developing nations, that is, the large scale technology can be adapted to the smaller markets of such nations. He finds that 'some entrepreneurs have found a niche for small scale technology' and that they need not be overwhelmed by the MNEs based in large industrialized nations. This is a good hypothesis which cries out for some empirical verification (like many other statements in the book — in fact, the main shortcoming of the book is the lack of empirical work reported, a factor which is perhaps not too surprising given the new ground covered by most of the authors).

The third theme running through several of the essays is the role of the government in fostering outward FDI and in the more familiar area of regulating inward flows of FDI. Diaz-Alejandro places most emphasis on the large public sector, common to Latin American nations, and draws the interesting implication that this has for state-owned MNEs. He also identifies the 'symbiotic relation between the state and large private or public enterprises' which raises the interesting implication that the MNE of a small nation will take on the political hue of its government. The MNE is not always a vehicle for capitalism but may be a result of state socialism. Either type of MNE can contribute to development. Diaz-Alejandro does not argue this point directly, but it appears to be implicit in his paper. One point he does make, which may surprise some readers, is that Latin American MNEs 'can be a positive force in the region's development, if encouraged in a selective and rational fashion'.

In a comment on Wells's paper, Steve Kobrin also dwells on the vital importance of political factors in explaining FDI. He gives a good summary of the literature on the political economy of the MNE with its emphasis on dependency, control and power. He states, correctly, that MNEs are 'significant transnational political actors in their own right' and draws the implication that they have not used their power to foster a redistribution of world income. On a brighter note, Kobrin advances the argument that MNEs based in small (and especially developing) nations may face fewer political problems than traditional MNEs. Unfortunately the MNEs from small nations are unlikely to be as efficient as those from major industrialized nations.

In conclusion, we are again confronted with the familiar trade-off between equity and efficiency. This trade-off is, of course, at the heart of economic theory so we cannot expect a book on the MNE to solve it. The contribution of this volume is its primary focus on issues of economics and efficiency, with a detailed evaluation of the role of the MNEs based in small nations. While the MNE cannot be expected to serve as a development agency (for this is the job of the government), it has been shown that the MNE is an efficient institution which responds to exogenous market imperfections. The MNE can be adapted to serve as an intermediary in the transfer of technology and can help to equalize the economic opportunities between poor and rich nations. In this way the MNE serves to promote the growth and development of all nations.

Note

1. This section first appeared in *Economic Development and Cultural Change* vol. 28, no. 4 (July 1980): 871-5. Reprinted with permission.

8 CONCLUSIONS: THE FUTURE OF INTERNALIZATION

This book has examined the nature and structure of the multinational enterprise, the dominant institution of the modern world. We have attempted to find out why the multinational enterprise is so important and we have tried to develop a theoretical explanation for its vitality. The theory focused upon the organization of the typical MNE and its internal market. It has been a difficult journey since the ramifications of internalization theory have been major and have led to conclusions which are frequently at variance with current public policy and thinking by both national governments and international organizations such as the United Nations. If the book has managed to challenge some of these current beliefs then the journey has been worthwhile.

The main objective of this book was to explain the theory of internalization and to explore some of its major implications. We have found that internalization is a theory of the multinational enterprise and that foreign direct investment is usually the preferred modality for servicing foreign markets. FDI is the method which allows the MNE its best chance of monitoring the use of its firm specific advantage. FDI is the device which lets the MNE maximize the potential returns on its valuable assets. FDI is frequently superior to licensing since the latter modality often involves the risk of dissipation of the firm specific advantage.

Milton Friedman has said that inflation is always and everywhere a monetary phenomenon. We can say that internalization is always a response to market imperfections and that both natural market failure and unnatural government regulations are everywhere. While world inflation has a monetarist cause we also now know that multinational enterprises exist due to worldwide market imperfections to which internal markets are the only viable economic response.

The chapter on the regulation of the multinationals examined the issue from the perspective of an advanced nation (Canada) and also from the viewpoint of less developed countries. In both cases it was found that regulation of the MNE is not called for. Indeed the MNE is a response to previous attempts by governments to impose restrictions on the market, either by using tariffs to protect indigenous industry or some other regulation to restrict foreign competition. Regulation is always inefficient. Multinationals are always efficient.

To be more precise, multinationals are efficient if the market imperfections (which they overcome by the creation of an internal market) are assumed to be external to the firm. Such exogenous market imperfections stem as much from regulations as they do from natural market failure. As long as governments persist in intervention in the marketplace there will remain incentives for internalization. Since the modern world is characterized by a great volume of market imperfections the future study of internalization can be predicted to remain a fertile one. Indeed, the multinational enterprise itself has a good future. The internal market of the multinational will be with us for a long time yet.

The performance of the MNE was examined in Chapter 7. No evidence was found of excessive profits being earned by the 50 largest US multinationals or the 50 largest non-US multinationals. The mean return on equity for both groups of firms is not significantly different from the all industry mean return on equity of some 12 to 13 per cent over the 1970-9 period. There are a few individual cases of excess profits being earned by some MNEs but these are almost exactly offset by unprofitable MNEs, especially in the European sector. Another chapter also argued that the majority of R and D is centralized in the parent MNE and some empirical evidence reported implied that the Canadian subsidiaries of US MNEs did less R and D than their parents.

MNEs also enjoy the benefits of international diversification and can use transfer pricing. Both of these attributes stem from the use of an internal market specific to the MNE. The advantages of internalization are large but they are offset by costs of ongoing R and D, threats of knowledge dissipation and the costs of gaining the requisite information for successful FDI. Multinational banks based in Canada appear to have enjoyed similar net advantages of internalization since the rate of increase in profits has been positively related to their degree of foreign activity.

The theoretical chapters of this book have shown that FDI is just one of the possible modes of servicing a foreign market. The choice of FDI over alternatives such as exporting or licensing depends upon the relative net profits of each modality. Yet, in practice, FDI is usually the method chosen by the MNE, since exporting is denied by tariffs while licensing faces the risk of dissipation of the firm specific advantage.

While the choice of mode depends entirely upon the relative amounts of the normal and special costs it is the main theme of this book to argue for the predominance of the FDI modality. Exporting is frequently denied by tariff and non-tariff barriers. Licensing, and other contractual arrangements, are extremely difficult to negotiate. The FDI modality works because the internal market of the MNE is a mechanism that avoids contractual difficulties and tariff walls.

Data on the relative importance of the three modalities tend to demonstrate the importance of FDI. It accounted for about 54 per cent of total foreign sales in the USA in 1971 according to Buckley and Davis (1979). Licensing is only about 10 per cent and exports are the remaining 35 per cent of foreign sales. Licensing is important only in Japan, at 41 per cent of total foreign sales (FDI being 10 per cent and exports 50 per cent). In the EEC licensing in 1971 was about 7 per cent; EFTA, 11 per cent; in Canada, 9.7 per cent. While in all these areas it is probable that licensed sales are increasing as a proportion of all foreign sales it is unlikely that contractual agreements will replace FDI in the future as the major form of servicing foreign markets.

The models developed in this book have distinguished between firm specific and country specific advantages. The knowledge advantage of the MNE is best protected by the internal market of the MNE. Yet the development of the initial knowledge advantage, and the ongoing R and D required to generate new innovations, partly depended upon the technological base of the home nation itself. A country specific advantage in technology is associated frequently with home nation MNEs which act as instruments for the overseas propagation of the advantage. Over time the internal market of the MNE serves to distinguish it in a peculiar fashion from firms which merely utilize the country specific advantage in export activities.

The export mode is a satisfactory one when entry to foreign markets is relatively unrestricted. An exporting firm can retain an advantage in information or knowledge within itself just as readily as an MNE. Indeed (if transport costs are ignored) an exporter can achieve worldwide scale economies by trade alone. But foreign governments generally deny the exporting modality. They respond to indigenous pressure groups and erect tariffs and other protective devices. Then FDI can become a substitute for exporting. Successful FDI requires a knowledge advantage (of the nation or firm) to be exploited abroad by wholly controlled affiliates, linked up by an effective internal market.

Over time the comparative advantages of nations will change. This reveals itself in changes in the country specific factors, and ultimately in new firm specific advantages. It will be difficult for an MNE to survive as an innovator in a nation with a persistently declining stock of knowledge capital. Therefore we observe changes in the relative performance of US, Japanese and European based MNEs. These movements reflect variations and developments of the technological bases of their respective home nations.

Vernon (1980) attributes the decline of American industry to a change in worldwide factor costs, whereby US labour saving technology grew redundant as raw materials and capital became relatively more expensive than labour. American technology was fostered in a nation of relatively cheap energy and resources but as these factors suffered dramatic increases in price in the 1970s rival producers in Europe and Japan were able to offer more efficient innovations in these areas than were US companies which traditionally focused mainly on labour saving techniques.

Vernon advocates a better use by US management of their overseas affiliates. Information on foreign markets, tastes and advances in overseas technology need to be fed back to the centre. The internal network of the multinational enterprise can be adapted for such two way transmission of information. Given the predominance of US based MNEs, such a change in strategy at the firm level would generate a national advantage in appropriate technology and product lines that should permit America to compete more successfully with Europe and Japan. It is noteworthy that Vernon identifies the potential to improve the country specific advantage of the United States with the firm specific advantage of MNEs, where these firms use their internal markets to transmit information both ways.

The transmission of information through the internal network of the MNE serves to identify it as an agent for the nation. The USA is the principal and the MNE is the agent. The objective for the USA is to gain information on foreign markets and potentially important new innovations. The MNE serves as a conduit for this flow of information. The management team of the MNE can winnow the relevant information from the irrelevant and respond with new strategies. This process of using the internal market of the MNE serves to carry over a technological advantage to the US economy itself. Thereby the MNE is an agent for the transmission of information. The USA (or any other nation-state served by a similar group of MNEs) can recover its technological advantage as a nation by working with its MNEs.

We observe that, in the area of technology, firm specific factors are interrelated with country specific ones. The firm specific advantage of the US based MNE in knowledge (and especially in its technological components) is best utilized by its internal market. Yet the internal market of the MNE is not one-dimensional. The other attributes of internalization permit the MNE to work a two-way flow of information within itself. Its overseas affiliates can garnish information about foreign markets and changes in foreign host country specific factors. Thereby the internal market of the MNE serves as an information agent for the parent firm and US economy at large. The US business community, society itself, and government generates expectations that the MNE will make good use of its intelligence. In practice the MNE has a vested interest in making effective use of information about the country specific factors of potential rivals, since it cannot afford to become obsolete or ignore new trends and innovations overseas. Thus the internal market of MNEs links firm and country specific factors in an indis-soluble web of knowledge exchange.

In the future we can anticipate that governments of host nations will place more barriers in the way of FDI. Not content with barriers to trade (which deny the export mode) governments are likely to respond to domestic pressures to regulate and monitor equity forms of foreign involvement (which will deny the FDI mode). This will leave licensing, or some other types of contractual arrangements, as the only remaining mode. The increased role for such non-equity forms of foreign involve-ment should not be accepted without question. There are both practical difficulties in arranging suitable contracts and also theoretical welfare costs involved in the forced switch to this modality.

The practical difficulty arises from the very nature of a negotiated contract. If the MNE has a genuine firm specific advantage in knowledge then it is going to be reluctant to put this at risk when forced to take a local partner. While joint ventures are feasible for standardized tech-nologies they are much more difficult to arrange with MNEs who are scared of knowledge dissipation. The risk of dissipation implicit in a non-equity form of foreign involvement may be partly offset by special clauses in the contract which permit the MNE to retain some control. Such an intermediate form of involvement may be forced upon MNEs as host nation-states move to restrict FDI.

The welfare costs of new restrictions on FDI arise due to the distortions imposed upon the choice of entry decision of the foreign (and also domestic) firms. Any government regulation to monitor, review, or otherwise restrict FDI drives a wedge between the relevant foreign and domestic price ratios, which should alone determine the foreign investment decision. In the same manner that a tariff distorts the relative price of tradeable to non-tradeable goods, and thereby reduces the economic welfare of a nation, any other regulatory device imposes welfare losses.

While it is hard to conceive of any Pareto optimal nations in the world at present, the point remains that, as a limiting case, free trade is efficient. Similarly, FDI can be an efficient mode when exporting has been denied to a firm. But a contractual arrangement is a deal. It is unlikely to ever approximate the efficiency of an internal market (used for FDI) or the regular market (used for free trade). Therefore, as the world is driven towards more and more government intervention in the international investment decision there will emerge an impossible phalanx of market imperfections to which the internal market and FDI may not be permitted to respond. The resulting welfare losses of inefficient contractual arrangements will be hard to live with. If the losses are as great as internalization theory predicts then, ultimately, there may be a relaxation of such restrictions in FDI (or the MNE may be clever enough to bypass them), so that there may be a revival of the MNE and its internal market.

The relevance of the theory of the MNE to less developed countries (LDCs) has been discussed by Agmon and Hirsch (1979). Their elegant Fisherian analysis is a valuable extension of the models of internalization discussed in this book. They argue that there are greater imperfections in the goods and factor markets of LDCs than in advanced nations, which implies that the LDCs have even more to gain from the presence of MNEs than do nations such as Canada and the UK.

In the early parts of this book it was stated that the MNE is an economic animal. This restricted analysis to the efficiency aspects of the MNE. This course of action has been followed throughout the work. At this late stage, however, it may be useful to address a few remarks to those more interested in the political economy of the MNE. The theory of internalization has several useful implications which may help to throw new light on the MNE. While it is beyond the scope of this book to engage in discussion of corporate ethics it is possible to review briefly the political and social impact of the MNE on host nations.

One of the main criticisms of the MNE from the viewpoint of political economy is the allegation that the MNE has excessive power. It is an organization that extends the influence of the home nation (often the USA) into the host nations. Sometimes it is suggested that the MNE is a vehicle for the furtherance of American hegemony. While it is correct to note that the method of FDI permits the MNE to spread the domain of its market to foreign nations it is only a half truth to conclude that this gives the MNE control over foreign nations. In practice, the governments of host nations remain sovereign. They may be open to influence by the MNE but it has to line up along with other pressure groups, many of which (such as protected indigenous industry and workers) may have interests at variance with the MNE.

Internalization is an economic device that lets the MNE overcome the high transactions costs of irregular or non-existent markets. The side product of an internal market is an efficient MNE. Yet the MNE is in the business of business. It is a corporation, not a political party or sovereign state in its own right. Its economic powers can be offset by the political powers of host nations, if they choose to do so. The MNE is forced to respond to its external political and social environment. The ability of the MNE to influence its environment is constrained by its need to specialize in ongoing R and R to maintain its firm specific advantage, without which it would become a paper tiger.

As well as criticism of its political dominance over host nations the MNE is also criticized on social grounds. It is accused of fostering worldwide consumerism to the extent that American cultural and environmental values (or rather lack of them) are imposed on host nations. Yet a relevant basic principle of economics is that the consumers own their demand functions. While the MNE can attempt to influence host nation demand it is eventually restricted in these efforts by its role as a producer. The MNE is not the consumer. Ultimately the consumers have independence and are sovereign. If they do not really want the production of the MNE they are not forced to purchase its products.

Thus the MNE needs to be constantly aware of the risks it runs in foreign nations if it appears to become overbearing and a threat to the host nation. When the consumers of the foreign nation adopt an attitude hostile to the MNE there is an inevitable reaction signalled by the introduction of restrictive host nation legislation. The governments of host nations are more responsive to their indigenous electorates than to foreign firms. The nation-state is not dead. Rather the host nation government is a countervailing force to the power of the MNE and is well able to protect its domain.

International organizations such as the UN and EEC can improve the environment for international business. They can do this by using their influence and regulations in a beneficial manner to help reduce the political risk facing the MNE in host nations, especially in developing nations. If such a spirit of co-operation between nation-states can be fostered by international organizations the needs of the MNE will be easier to meet. The North-South debate is likely to dominate the 1980s and the role of the MNE in this massive issue of world income redistribution will be a significant one, even though this role should be confined to efficiency aspects. A greater spirit of political understanding may occur in the developed nations of the North as they face persistent problems of unemployment, inflation and deindustrialization. The prospects for such harmonization of political objectives are not so good for the less developed nations of the South. Indeed, their growing hostility towards the MNE may keep on increasing and hinder their prospects for growth. On balance, there may be some reduction of government control and regulation of the MNE, since its major sales are between developed nations. This slight reduction in market imperfections is unlikely to destroy the incentives for internal markets in the future.

The labour unions of both home and host nations are restricted in their ability to deal with the MNE, lacking, as they do, any organization comparable to the internal market of the MNE. The internal market permits the management team of the MNE to cross national boundaries and gives it a chance to arbitrage the labour markets of various nations. While the MNE can cross the boundaries of nation states in its industrial relations, the trade unions of most countries are pretty much restricted in their operations and bargaining to their home nation. While unions are willing to exchange information on international business and economic trends there are excessive costs involved in the formation of true international trade unions that could oppose the perceived power of MNEs in the labour markets of the world. Even in the US-Canadian case, where international (i.e. US) unions have traditionally organized many of the Canadian subsidiaries of US MNEs, there has been evidence in recent years of increased nationalism at the local level, so that newly formed, or revamped, domestic Canadian unions now compete for members with the US international unions. If trade unions become better integrated in the future then there will be additional pressure placed on the operations of the MNE. Then its performance may well suffer, since we have observed that MNEs are not earning excess profits, even given the present situation of their industrial relations advantage.

When a book takes as its focus one organization there is a danger that the importance of that organization can be exaggerated. In these concluding remarks I am attempting to minimize this problem by stating explicitly that the MNE is a creature of its environment. It has to live within the constraints imposed by the world system of nation-states, taxation and regulation. The theory of the MNE is still in its infancy but it can probably make its most useful advances at this stage of its development by taking the environmental factors as exogenous. This analysis of the internal markets of the MNE has proceeded in this manner. The extension of the theory of the MNE by making environmental variables endogenous is a task left for the future.

BIBLIOGRAPHY

Agmon, Tamir, and Hirsch, Seev. 'Multinational Corporations and the Developing Economies: Potential Gains in a World of Imperfect Markets and Uncertainty.' *Oxford Bulletin of Economics and Statistics* 41 (November 1979): 333-4

Agmon, Tamir, and Kindleberger, Charles P., eds. *Multinationals from Small Countries.* Cambridge, Mass.: MIT Press, 1977

Agmon, Tamir, and Lessard, Donald R. 'Investor Recognition of Corporate International Diversification.' *Journal of Finance* 32 (September 1977): 1049-55

Aharoni, Yair. *The Foreign Investment Decision Process.* Boston: Harvard Business School, 1966

Alexander, Judith A. 'Research and Development Activity in Domestic and Foreign Controlled Industries.' Mimeographed. Centre for International Business Studies, Dalhousie University: Discussion Paper in International Business No. 4 (August 1980)

Aliber, Robert Z. 'A Theory of Direct Foreign Investment.' In *The International Corporation.* Edited by Charles P. Kindleberger. Cambridge, Mass.: MIT Press, 1970

_____ . *Exchange Risk and Corporate International Finance.* London and Basingstoke: Macmillan, 1978a

_____ . 'The Integration of National Financial Markets: A Review of Theory and Findings.' *Weltwirtschaftliches Archiv* 114 (September 1978b): 448-79

Allen, Deborah, and Giddy, Ian H. 'Measuring the Economic Impact of Differential Treatment of Foreign and Domestic Banks.' Mimeographed. Office of the Comptroller of The Currency, Washington, DC (July 1979)

Ayarslan, Solmaz D. 'Foreign Exchange Rate Changes and the Stock Prices of U.S. Multinational Corporations.' Mimeographed. Presented at the annual meetings of the North American Economic Studies Association, Denver, Colorado (September 1980)

Bergsten, C. Fred, Horst, Thomas, and Moran, Theodore H. *American Multinationals and American Interests.* Washington, DC: The Brookings Institution, 1978

Biersteker, Thomas J. *Distortion or Development? Contending Perspectives on the Multinational Corporation.* Cambridge, Mass.: MIT Press, 1978

165

Bloch, Harry. 'Prices, Costs and Profits in Canadian Manufacturing: The Influence of Tariffs and Concentration.' *Canadian Journal of Economics* 7 (November 1974): 564-610

Bones, Herman P. 'Are Foreign Subsidiaries More Innovative?' *Foreign Investment Review* 3 (Spring 1980): 20-3

Bonin, Bernard. 'Licensing, Joint Ventures and the Transfer of Technology.' Mimeographed paper to The First Canadian-Hungarian Economic Roundtable, Budapest (October 1979)

Booth, E.J.R., and Jensen, O.W. 'Transfer Prices in The Global Corporation Under Internal and External Constraints.' *Canadian Journal of Economics* 10 (August 1977): 434-46

Britton, John N.H., and Gilmour, James M. *The Weakest Link – A Technological Perspective on Canadian Industrial Underdevelopment.* Ottawa: Science Council of Canada, 1978

Brown, W.R. 'Islands of Conscious Power: MNCs in the Theory of The Firm.' *MSU Business Topics* (Summer 1976): 37-54

Bruck, Nicholas K., and Lees, Francis A. 'Foreign Investment, Capital Controls and the Balance of Payments.' *The Bulletin*. New York University Graduate School of Business Administration Institute of Finance No. 48-9 (April 1968)

Buckley, Peter, and Casson, Mark. *The Future of the Multinational Enterprise.* Basingstoke and London: Macmillan, 1976

——. 'The Optimal Timing of a Foreign Direct Investment.' University of Reading Discussion Papers in International Investment and Business Studies No. 48 (February 1980). Forthcoming, *Economic Journal* (1981)

Buckley, Peter J., and Davis, Howard. 'The Place of Licensing in the Theory and Practice of Foreign Operations.' Mimeographed. University of Reading Discussion Papers in International Investment and Business Studies No. 47 (November 1979)

Casson, Mark. *Alternatives to The Multinational Enterprise.* London: Macmillan, 1979

Caves, Richard E. 'International Corporations: The Industrial Economics of Foreign Investment.' *Economica* 38 (February 1971): 1-27

——. *International Trade, International Investment and Imperfect Markets.* International Finance Section, Princeton University: Special Papers in International Economics No. 10 (November 1974)

Coase, Ronald H. 'The Nature of the Firm.' *Economica* (1937): 386-405. Reprinted in *Readings in Price Theory*. Edited by G. Stigler and K. Boulding. Homewood, Illinois: Irwin, 1952

Copithorne, L.W. 'International Corporate Transfer Prices and

Government Policy.' *Canadian Journal of Economics* 4 (August
   1971): 324-41
Corden, Max. *Trade Policy and Economic Welfare.* Oxford: Oxford
   University Press, 1974
Cornell, Bradford. 'Spot Rates, Forward Rates and Exchange Market
   Efficiency.' *Journal of Financial Economics* 5 (August 1977): 55-65
Daly, Donald J. 'Weak Links in the Weakest Link.' *Canadian Public
   Policy* 5 (Summer 1979): 307-17
Davidson, W.H., and McFetridge, Donald G. 'International Technology
   and the Theory of the Firm.' Mimeographed. Department of
   Economics, Carleton University (1980)
Dean, James W., and Grubel, Herbert G. 'Multinational Banking: Theory
   and Regulation.' In *Issues in Financial Regulation.* Edited by Franklin
   R. Edwards. New York: McGraw-Hill, 1979
Dean, James W., and Schwindt, Richard. 'Bank Act Revision in Canada:
   Past and Potential Effects on Market Structure and Competition.'
   Banca Nazionale del Lavoro-Quarterly Review 116 (March 1976):
   19-49
Diaz-Alejandro, Carlos F. 'Delinking North and South: Unshackled or
   Unhinged?' In *Rich and Poor Nations in the World Economy.* Edited
   by Albert Fishlow *et al.*, New York: McGraw-Hill, 1978
Dufey, Gunter, and Giddy, Ian H. *The International Money Market.*
   Englewood Cliffs: Prentice-Hall, 1978
Dukes, Roland. 'Forecasting Exchange Gains (Losses) and Security
   Market Response to FASB Statement No. 8.' In *Exchange Risk and
   Exposure.* Edited by Richard M. Levich, and Clas G. Wihlborg.
   Lexington, Mass.: D.C. Heath, 1980
Dunning, John H. 'The Determinants of International Production.'
   Oxford Economic Papers 25 (November 1973): 289-336
____. 'Trade, Location of Economic Activity and the MNE: A Search
   for an Eclectic Approach.' In *The International Allocation of
   Economic Activity. Proceedings of a Nobel Symposium held at
   Stockholm.* Edited by Bertil Ohlin *et al.* London: Macmillan, 1977
____. 'Explaining Changing Patterns of International Production: In
   Defence of The Eclectic Theory.' *Oxford Bulletin of Economics and
   Statistics* 41 (November 1979): 269-96
Eastman, H.C., and Stykolt, S. *The Tariff and Competition in Canada.*
   Toronto: Macmillan, 1967
Eden, Lorraine. 'Vertically Integrated Multinationals: A Microeconomic
   Analysis.' *Canadian Journal of Economics* 11 (August 1978): 534-46
Elliott, J.W. 'The Expected Return to Equity and International Asset

Prices.' *Journal of Financial and Quantitative Analysis* 13 (December 1978): 987-1002

Fishlow, Albert, *et al. Rich and Poor Nations in the World Economy.* New York: McGraw-Hill, 1978

Folks Jr, William R., and Evans, Thomas G. 'The Impact of FASB Statement Number 8 on Corporate Exchange Risk Management.' In *Exchange Risk and Exposure.* Edited by Richard M. Levich and Clas Wihlborg. Lexington, Mass.: D.C. Heath, 1980

Frankl, Roslyn. 'A Cross-Section Analysis of Research and Development Intensity in Canadian Industries with Particular Reference to Foreign Control.' Mimeographed. Canada: Industry, Trade and Commerce: Economic Policy and Analysis Division (May 1979)

Galbraith, Jack A. *Canadian Banking.* Toronto: The Ryerson Press, 1970

Giddy, Ian H. 'Devaluations, Revaluations and Stock Market Prices.' Unpublished PhD dissertation, University of Michigan, 1974

——. 'The Cost of Capital in The International Firm.' Columbia University Graduate School of Business Research Working Paper (August 1977a)

——. 'Exchange Risk: Whose View?' *Financial Management* 6 (Summer 1977b): 23-32

——. 'The Demise of the Product Cycle Model in International Business Theory.' *Columbia Journal of World Business* 13 (Spring 1978): 90-7

Giddy, Ian, and Rugman, Alan M. 'A Model of Trade, Foreign Direct Investment and Licensing.' Mimeographed. Graduate School of Business, Columbia University (December 1979)

Globerman, S. 'Market Structure and R and D in Canadian Manufacturing Industries.' *Quarterly Review of Economics and Business* 13 (1973): 59-67

Gould, J. 'Internal Pricing in Firms Where There are Costs of Using an Outside Market.' *Journal of Business* 37 (1964): 61-7

Gray, H. Peter. *International Trade, Investments and Payments.* Boston: Houghton Mifflin, 1979

Grubel, Herbert G. 'Internationally Diversified Portfolios: Welfare Gains and Capital Flows.' *American Economic Review* 58 (December 1968): 1299-314

——. *International Economics.* Homewood, Illinois: Irwin, 1977a

——. 'A Theory of Multinational Banking.' *Banca Nazionale del Lavoro Quarterly Review* 123 (1977b): 349-63

Hewitt, Gary K. 'Research and Development Performed Abroad by U.S. Manufacturing Multinationals.' *Kyklos* 33 (June 1980a): 308-27

____. 'Research and Development Performed in Canada by American Manufacturing Multinationals.' Mimeographed. Centre for International Business Studies, Dalhousie University. Discussion Paper in International Business No. 3 (August, 1980b)

Hirsch, Seev. 'An International Trade and Investment Theory of the Firm.' *Oxford Economic Papers* 28 (July 1976): 258-70

Hirschleifer, J. 'On the Economics of Transfer Pricing.' *Journal of Business* 29 (1956): 172-84

Hochmuth, Milton. 'Multinationals, Transnationals and Now Conationals.' In *European Research in International Business*, pp. 169-87. Edited by Michael Ghertman and James Leontides. Amsterdam: North Holland, 1978

Hood, Neil, and Young, Stephen. *The Economics of Multinational Enterprise.* London: Longman, 1979

Horst, Thomas. 'The Theory of the Multinational Firm: Optimal Behaviour Under Different Tariff and Tax Rates.' *Journal of Political Economy* 79 (1971): 1059-72

____. 'The Simple Analytics of Multi-National Firm Behaviour.' In *International Trade and Money.* Edited by Michael B. Connolly and Alexander Swoboda. Toronto: University of Toronto Press, 1973

____. 'Theory of the Firm'. In *Economic Analysis and the Multinational Enterprise.* Edited by John H. Dunning. London: Allen and Unwin, 1974

____. 'American Taxation of Multinational Corporations.' *American Economic Review* 67 (June 1977): 376-89

Howe, J.D., and McFetridge, D.G. 'The Determinants of R and D Expenditures.' *Canadian Journal of Economics* IX (February 1976): 57-61

Hufbauer, Gary C. 'The Multinational Corporation and Direct Investment.' In *International Trade and Finance*, pp. 253-320. Edited by Peter B. Kenen. New York: Cambridge University Press, 1975

Hughes, John S., Logue, Dennis E., and Sweeney, Richard J. 'Corporate International Diversification and Market Assigned Measures of Risk and Diversification.' *Journal of Financial and Quantitative Analysis* (November 1975): 627-38

Hymer, Stephen H. *The International Operations of National Firms: A Study of Direct Foreign Investment.* Cambridge: Mass.: MIT Press, 1976

____. *The Multinational Corporation: A Radical Approach.* Edited by Robert B. Cohen *et al.* Cambridge: Cambridge University Press, 1979

Johnson, Harry G. 'The Efficiency and Welfare Implications of the International Corporation.' In *The International Corporation*, pp. 35-56. Edited by Charles P. Kindleberger. Cambridge, Mass.: MIT Press, 1970

_____. *Aspects of the Theory of Tariffs.* London: Allen and Unwin, 1971

Khoury, Sarkis. *The Dynamics of International Banking.* New York: Praeger, 1980

Kindleberger, Charles P. *American Business Abroad: Six Lectures on Direct Investment.* New Haven and London: Yale University Press, 1969

Kircher, Donald. 'Now the Transnational Enterprise.' *Harvard Business Review* (March-April 1964)

Knickerbocker, Frederick T. *Oligopolistic Reaction and Multinational Enterprise.* Boston: Harvard University Press, 1973

Kojima, Kiyoshi. *Direct Foreign Investment: A Japanese Model of Multinational Business Operations.* London: Croom Helm, 1978

Kotz, David M. *Bank Control of Large Corporations in the United States.* Berkeley: University of California Press, 1978

Lall, Sanjaya. 'Transfer Pricing by Multinational Manufacturing Firms.' *Oxford Bulletin of Economics and Statistics* 35 (August 1973): 173-95

Lamfalussy, Alexandre. *Investment and Growth in Mature Economies.* Oxford: Basil Blackwell and Mott, 1961

Leff, Nathaniel H. 'Industrial Organization and Entrepreneurship in the Developing Countries: The Economic Groups.' *Economic Development and Cultural Change* 26 (July 1978): 661-75

Lessard, Donald R. 'Transfer Prices, Taxes and Financial Markets: Implications of Internal Financial Transfers within the Multinational Corporation.' In *Research in International Business and Finance*, Vol. 1: *The Economic Effect of Multinational Corporations*. Edited by Robert G. Hawkins, Greenwich, Conn.: JAI Press, 1979

Levich, Richard M. 'On the Efficiency of Markets for Foreign Exchange.' In *International Economic Policy: An Assessment of Theory and Evidence.* Edited by Rudiger Dornbusch and Jacob A. Frenkel. Baltimore, Maryland: Johns Hopkins University Press, 1979

Levich, Richard M., and Wihlborg, Clas G., eds. *Exchange Risk and Exposure.* Lexington, Mass.: D.C. Heath, 1980

Magee, Stephen P. 'Multinational Corporations, the Industry Technology Cycle and Development.' *Journal of World Trade Law* 11 (July-August 1977a): 297-321

_____. 'Information and the Multinational Corporation: An Appropriability Theory of Direct Foreign Investment.' In *The New International Economic Order*, pp. 317-40. Edited by J.N. Bhagwati. Cambridge, Mass.: MIT Press, 1977b

Martin, F., Swan, N., Bankes, I., Barker, G., and Beaudry, R. *The*

Interregional Diffusion of Innovation in Canada. Ottawa: Economic Council of Canada, 1979

Mathewson, G.F., and Quirin, G.D. *Fiscal Transfer Pricing in Multinational Corporations.* Toronto: University of Toronto Press, 1979

Mazzolini, Renato. *Government Controlled Enterprises: International Strategic and Policy Decision.* New York: John Wiley, 1979

McFetridge, D.G. *Government Support of Scientific Research and Development: An Economic Analysis.* Toronto: University of Toronto Press, 1977

McFetridge, D.G., and Weatherly, L.J. *Notes on the Economics of Large Firm Size.* Study No. 20, Royal Commission on Corporate Concentration. Ottawa, 1977

McManus, J. 'The Theory of the International Firm.' In *The Multinational Firm and The Nation State.* Edited by G. Paquet. Toronto: Collier-Macmillan, 1972

Mintz, Jack M. *The Measure of Rates of Return in Canadian Banking.* Hull, Quebec: Economic Council of Canada, 1979

Negandhi, Anant R. (ed.) *Functioning of the Multinational Corporation: A Global Comparative Study.* New York: Pergamon, 1980

Nieckels, Lars. *Transfer Pricing in Multinational Firms.* Stockholm: Almqvist and Wiksell, 1976

Orr, Dale. 'The Determinants of Entry: A Study of the Canadian Manufacturing Industries.' *Review of Economics and Statistics* (February 1974): 58-66

Pattison, J.C. *Financial Markets and Foreign Ownership.* Toronto: Ontario Economic Council, 1978

Perlmutter, H. 'The Tortuous Evolution of the Multinational Corporation.' *Columbia Journal of World Business* 4 (January-February 1969): 9-18

Prachowny, Martin F., and Richardson, J. David. 'Testing a Life-Cycle Hypothesis of the Balance of Payments Effects of Multinational Corporations.' *Economic Inquiry* XIII: 1 (March 1975): 81-98

Robbins, Sidney M., and Stobaugh, Robert B. *Money in The Multinational Enterprise.* New York: Basic Books, 1973

Robock, S.H., Simmonds, K., and Zwick, J. *International Business and Multinational Enterprises.* Homewood, Illinois: Irwin, 1977

Ronstadt, Robert. *Research and Development Abroad by U.S. Multinationals.* New York: Praeger, 1977

Rosenbluth, Gideon. 'The Relation Between Foreign Control and Concentration in Canadian Industry.' *Canadian Journal of Economics* 3 (February 1970): 14-38

Rugman, Alan M. 'Motives for Foreign Investment: The Market
   Imperfections and Risk Diversification Hypotheses.' *Journal of
   World Trade Law* 9 (September-October 1975): 567-73
_____. 'Risk Reduction by International Diversification.' *Journal of
   International Business Studies* 7 (Fall 1976): 75-80
_____. 'Risk, Direct Investment and International Diversification.' *Welt-
   wirtschaftliches Archiv* 113 (September 1977a): 485-500
_____. 'International Diversification by Financial and Direct Investment.'
   Journal of Economics and Business 30 (October 1977b): 31-7
_____. *International Diversification and the Multinational Enterprise.*
   Lexington: D.C. Heath, 1979
_____. 'Internalization as a General Theory of Foreign Direct Investment.'
   Weltwirtschaftliches Archiv 116 (June 1980a): 365-79
_____. *Multinationals in Canada: Theory, Performance and Economic
   Impact.* Boston: Martinus Nijhoff, 1980b
_____. 'A New Theory of the Multinational Enterprise: International-
   ization Versus Internalization.' *Columbia Journal of World Business*
   (Spring 1980c): 23-9
_____. 'Internalization and the Transfer of Technology to Canada.'
   Mimeographed. Centre for International Business Studies, Dalhousie
   University. Discussion Paper in International Business No. 1 (July
   1980d)
_____. 'A Test of Internalization Theory.' Mimeographed. Centre for
   International Business Studies, Dalhousie University: Discussion Paper
   in International Business No. 5 (August 1980e)
_____. 'Transfer Pricing Problems of Multinational Corporations.' In
   Functioning of The Multinational Corporation, pp. 51-76. Edited by
   Anant R. Negandhi, New York: Pergamon, 1980f
_____. 'Implications of the Theory of Internalization for Corporate
   International Finance.' Paper presented to the Annual Meeting of the
   Financial Management Association, Boston, October 1979. Forth-
   coming in *California Management Review* 23 (Winter 1980g)
Safarian, A.E. *Foreign Ownership of Canadian Industry.* McGraw-Hill,
   1966. 2nd edition: University of Toronto Press, 1973
_____. 'Foreign Ownership and Industrial Behaviour.' *Canadian Public
   Policy* V (Summer 1979): 318-35
Scherer, F.M. *Industrial Market Structure and Economic Performance.*
   Chicago: Rand-McNally, 1970
Science Council of Canada. *Forging the Links: A Technology Policy for
   Canada.* Ottawa: Science Council of Canada, 1979
_____. *Multinationals and Industrial Strategy: The Role of World Product*

Mandates. Ottawa: Science Council of Canada, 1980

Senchack, Andrew H., and Beedles, William. 'Indirect International Diversification Through U.S. Multinational Firms.' *Journal of the Midwest Finance Association* (1978): 145-56

Shapiro, Alan. 'Financial Structure and The Cost of Capital in The Multinational Corporation.' *Journal of Financial and Quantitative Analysis* 13 (June 1978): 211-26

Shapiro, Daniel M. *Foreign and Domestic Firms in Canada.* Toronto: Butterworths, 1980

Solomon, Lewis D. *Multinational Corporations and the Emerging World Order.* Port Washington, New York: Kennikat Press, 1978

Statistics Canada. *Annual Review of Science Statistics.* Ottawa: Statistics Canada, Education, Science and Culture Division. Catalogue No 13-212 Annual

____. *Corporations and Labour Unions Return Act.* Part 1 – Corporations. Ottawa: Statistics Canada. Catalogue No. 61-210 Annual

Teece, David J. *The Multinational Corporation and The Resource Cost of International Technology Transfer.* Cambridge, Mass.: Ballinger, 1976

Telesio, Piero. *Technology, Licensing and Multinational Enterprises.* New York: Praeger, 1979

Tschoegl, Adrian E. 'Essays in Foreign Direct Investment in Banking.' Unpublished PhD Dissertation, Sloan School of Management, MIT, 1980

United Nations, Economic and Social Council. *Transnational Corporations in World Development: A Re-Examination.* United Nations: Commission of Transnational Corporations, 78-05492, March 1978

Vaitsos, Constantine. *Intercountry Income Distribution and Transnational Enterprise.* Oxford: Oxford University Press, 1974

Vaupel, James W., and Curhan, Joan P. *The Making of Multinational Enterprise: A Sourcebook of Tables Based on a Study of 187 Major U.S. Manufacturing Corporations.* Boston: Harvard Business School, 1969

Vernon, Raymond. 'International Investment and International Trade in The Product Cycle.' *Quarterly Journal of Economics* 30 (May 1966): 190-207

____. *Sovereignty at Bay: The Multinational Spread of United States Enterprises.* New York: Basic Books, 1971

____. *Storm Over the Multinationals: The Real Issues.* London and Basingstoke: Macmillan, 1977

____. 'Gone are the Cash Cows of Yesteryear.' *Harvard Business Review*

58 (November-December 1980): 150-5

Vernon, Raymond, and Davidson, William H. 'Foreign Production of Technology-Intensive Products by U.S.-Based Multinational Enterprises.' Mimeographed. Harvard Business School, January 1979

Walters, Kenneth D., and Monsen, Joseph. 'State-Owned Business Abroad: New Competitive Threat.' *Harvard Business Review* 57 (March-April 1979): 160-70

Williamson, Oliver E. *Markets and Hierarchies: Analysis and Antitrust Implications: A Study in the Economics of Internal Organizations.* New York: Free-Press, Macmillan, 1975

Wriggens, W. Howard, and Adler-Karlsson, Gunnar. *Reducing Global Inequities.* New York: McGraw-Hill, 1978

INDEX